Seal of the State of Tennessee

CHRONOLOGY AND DOCUMENTARY HANDBOOK OF THE STATE OF
TENNESSEE

ROBERT I. VEXLER

State Editor

WILLIAM F. SWINDLER

Series Editor

1979 OCEANA PUBLICATIONS, INC./ Dobbs Ferry, New York

Library of Congress Cataloging in Publication Data

Main entry under title:

Chronology and documentary handbook of the State of
    Tennessee.

   (Chronologies and documentary handbooks of the
States; 42)
   Bibliography: p.
   Includes index.
   SUMMARY: Contains a chronology of events in Tennessee
from 1540 to 1977, biographical sketches of prominent
citizens, and selected documents pertinent to Tennessee
history.
   1. Tennessee—History—Chronology.   2. Tennessee—
Biography.   3. Tennessee—History—Sources.
[1. Tennessee—History]   I. Vexler, Robert I.
II. Series.
F436.5.C48   976.8'002'02   78-26261
ISBN 0-379-16167-2

© Copyright 1979 by Oceana Publications, Inc.

All rights reserved. No part of this publication may be reproduced or transmitted in any
form or by any means, electronic or mechanical, including photocopy, recording,
xerography, or any information storage and retrieval system, without permission in
writing from the publisher.

Manufactured in the United States of America

TABLE OF CONTENTS

INTRODUCTION ix

CHRONOLOGY (1540-1977) 1

BIOGRAPHICAL DIRECTORY 31

PROMINENT PERSONALITIES 69

FIRST STATE CONSTITUTION 75

SELECTED DOCUMENTS 89
   Tennessee During the Civil War 91
   The Battle of Chickamauga, September
      19-20, 1863 107
   Cotton Patch Life In Tennessee 119
   Basic Facts 139
   Map of Congressional Districts 140

SELECTED BIBLIOGRAPHY 141

NAME INDEX 143

ACKNOWLEDGMENT

Special recognition should be accorded Melvin Hecker, whose research has made a valuable contribution to this volume.

Thanks to my wife, Francine, in appreciation of her help in the preparation of this work.

Thanks also to my children, David and Melissa, without whose patience and understanding I would have been unable to devote the considerable time necessary for completing the state chronology series.

I also wish to acknowledge the scholarly research grant given to me by Pace University. This greatly eased the technical preparation of this work.

Robert I. Vexler
Pace University

INTRODUCTION

This projected series of *Chronologies and Documentary Handbooks of the States* will ultimately comprise fifty separate volumes—one for each of the states of the Union. Each volume is intended to provide a concise ready reference to basic data on the state, and to serve as a starting point for more extended study as the individual user may require. Hopefully, it will be a guidebook for a better informed citizenry - students, civic and service organizations, professional and business personnel, and others.

The editorial plan for the *Handbook* series falls into six divisions: (1) a chronology of selected events in the history of the state; (2) a short biographical directory of the principal public officials, e.g., governors, Senators and Representatives; (3) a short biographical directory of prominent personalities of the state (for most states); (4) the first state constitution; (5) the text of some representative documents illustrating main currents in the political, economic, social or cultural history of the state; and (6) a selected bibliography for those seeking further or more detailed information. Most of the data found in the present volume, in fact, have been taken from one or another of these references.

The current constitutions of all fifty states, as well as the federal Constitution, are regularly kept up to date in the definitive collection maintained by the Legislative Drafting Research of Columbia University and published by the publisher of the present series of *Handbooks*. These texts are available in most major libraries under the title, *Constitutions of the United States: National and State,* in two volumes, with a companion volume, the *Index Digest of State Constitutions.*

Finally, the complete collection of documents illustrative of the constitutional development of each state, from colonial or territorial status up to the current constitution as found in the Columbia University collection, is being prepared for publication in a multi-volume series by the present series editor. Whereas the present series of *Handbooks* is intended for a wide range of interested citizens, the series of annotated constitutional materials in the volumes of *Sources and Documents of U.S. Constitutions* is primarily for the specialist in government, history or law. This is not to suggest that the general citizenry may not profit equally from referring to these materials; rather it points up the separate purpose of the *Handbooks*, which is to guide the user of these and other sources of authoritative information with which he may systematically enrich his knowledge of this state and its place in the American Union.

William J. Swindler
John Marshall Professor of Law
College of William and Mary
Series Editor

Robert I. Vexler
Associate Professor of History
Pace University
Series Associate Editor

Agriculture and Commerce
State Motto

CHRONOLOGY

1540   Hernando de Soto led the first white expedition into the Tennessee region.

1566   Juan Pedro and a group of Spaniards built a fort near the site of present-day Chattanooga.

1584   The region of Tennessee was included in the English grant made to Sir Walter Raleigh.

1673   James Needham and Gabriel Arthur explored the eastern portion of Tennessee for Virginia. Louis Joliet and Jacques Marquette explored the western part of the state for France.

1682   Robert Cavalier, Sieur de la Salle, claimed Tennessee for France. He supervised construction of Fort Prud'homme near present-day Memphis at the mouth of the Hatchie River.

1714   Charles Charleville established a French trading post near the location of present-day Nashville.

1750   Dr. Thomas Walker led a group of Virginians into Tennessee. They reached the Cumberland River and mountains which they named in honor of the Duke of Cumberland.

1757   A group of South Carolinians constructed Fort Loudon on the Little Tennessee River, 30 miles north of present-day Knoxville. The fort was named in honor of John Campbell, Earl of Loudon.

1760   The Cherokee Indians captured Fort Loudon, killing the garrison and the nearby settlers.

1763   France surrendered all claims to the land east of the Mississippi River to Great Britain.

1766   November 18. Sumner County, with its seat at Gallatin, was created. It was named for Jethro Sumner who fought in the French and Indian War and later in the Revolution.

           Captain James Smith, leading a group of five people, including a mulatto slave, explored a large part of the state.

1768	The Iroquois Indians ceded their claims to Tennessee to the English.
	The first permanent white settlement was founded among the Watuga and Holston Rivers.
1771	A settlement was established near present-day Rogersville.
1772	Residents of the first two settlements met in a general convention to establish the Watauga Association.
	A settlement was created on the Nollichucky River.
1775	March 17. Colonel Richard Henderson and his associates eliminated the Indian title to an immense tract of land in the Cumberland Valley.
	The settlement on the Nollichacky River was forced to join the Watauga Association.
1776	The Territory of Tennessee was annexed to North Carolina as the Washington District. It became Washington County in 1777.
1777	November 15. At the session of the legislature Washington County was created, with Jonesboro and Johnson City as the county seats. The county was named for George Washington who was commander of all the Continental armies and later first President of the United States.
1779	James Robertson and a small group of settlers arrived at French Lick.
	October 18. Sullivan County was established. It was named for James Sullivan, member of the Continental Congress, federal Constitutional Convention and New Hampshire official.
1780	Tennesseans helped defeat the British at King's Mountain, South Carolina.
	Nashville settlers signed the Cumberland Compact. The settlement was originally called Nashborough.

CHRONOLOGY

1783 — April 18. Davidson and Greene Counties were established at the session of the legislature. Davidson, with Nashville as its seat, was named for William Lee Davidson who served in the Revolutionary War and was killed at the battle of Cowan's Pass on February 1, 1781.

Greene, with Greenville as its county seat, was named for Nathanael Greene who was a general in the Continental Army.

James Robertson was sent as a delegate to the North Carolina legislature.

1784 — August 23. A convention of the Watauga settlers met at Jonesborough where they named delegates to a second convention to establish a new state.

November. The second convention met but accomplished little. The delegates did form the short-lived state of Franklin.

North Carolina ceded the land which is now Tennessee to the federal government.

1785 — John Sevier became governor of the state of Franklin, serving in this capacity until 1788.

1786 — November 18. At the session of the legislature Hawkins County was created, with Rogersville as its seat. It was named for Benjamin Hawkins, United States Senator from North Carolina and Indian agents for the tribes south of the Ohio River.

1790 — Population: 35,691.

February 25. North Carolina ceded the region to the federal government again on condition that all general provisions of the Ordinance of 1787 apply except that which forbade slavery.

May 26. The territory south of the Ohio River was established.

August 7. William Blount was appointed governor of the territory. He served in the post until 1796.

1791   The <u>Knoxville Gazette</u> was published as the first paper in Tennessee.

1792   June 11. Jefferson and Knox Counties were created. Jefferson, with Dandridge as its seat, was named for Thomas Jefferson, author and signer of the Declaration of Independence, Secretary of State in the Administration of President George Washington, and later third President of the United States.

Knox, with Knoxville, as its seat, was named for Henry Knox, brigadier general of the Continental Army and Secretary of War in the Cabinet of President George Washington.

1794   September 10. The University of Tennessee received its first charter as Blount College in Knoxville. It became a state university in 1806 when a federal grant provided for two state universities. Blount was selected as the eastern institution. It became East Tennessee College in 1840, East Tennessee University in 1840 and the University of Tennessee in 1879.

September 27. Sevier County, with its seat at Sevierville, was established. It was named for John Sevier, first and third governor of Tennessee and United States Representative from Tennessee.

Washington and Tusculum College was founded at Greenville.

1795   July 11. Blount County, with Maryville as its seat, was created. It was named for William Blount, governor of the territory south of the Ohio River, Superintendent of Indian Affairs, and United States Senator from Tennessee.

1796   January 11. A state convention met to draft a constitution at Knoxville.

March 30. John Sevier, Democrat-Republican, became governor of Tennessee in which post he served until September 23, 1801.

April 9. Montgomery and Robertson Counties were created. Montgomery, with its seat at Clarksville, was named for James Montgomery who explored the Cumberland area and fought in a campaign against the Indians in 1794.

Robertson County, with its seat at Springfield, was named for James Robertson, an Indian fighter, founder of Nashborough, member of the Tennessee constitutional convention and state senator.

April 22. Grainger County, with Rutledge as its seat, was established. It was named for Mary Grainer, daughter of Colonel Caleb Grainger, who married Governor William Blount.

June 1. Tennessee was admitted to the Union as the 16th state.

July 7. Tennessee's United States Senator, William Blount, was the first person to be impeached by the United States House of Representatives for trying to stir up an Indian war. Blount was expelled from the Senate, but the impeachment was dismissed in 1799.

October 9. Cocke and Union Counties were created. Cocke, with its seat at Newport, was named for William Cocke who explored the region with Daniel Boone, was a member of the Virginia house of burgesses, a member of the Tennessee constitutional convention, United States Senator from Tennessee and later a member of the Mississippi legislature.

Union County has its seat at Maynardville.

1799   October 26. Smith, Williamson and Wilson Counties were established. Smith, with its seat at Carthage, was named for Daniel Smith, secretary of the Territory South of the Ohio River, member of the first Tennessee constitutional convention, and United States Senator from Tennessee.

Williamson, with Franklin as its seat, was named for Hugh Williamson, a physician, surgeon-general to the general troops of North Carolina during the Revolutionary War and United States Representative from North Carolina.

Wilson, with its county seat at Lebanon, was named for Daniel Wilson, who fought in the

Revolutionary War and was member and speaker of the Tennessee House of Representatives.

1800   Population: 105,602.

1801   September 23. Archibald Roane, Democrat-Republican, became governor of the state. He served in the office until September 23, 1803.

October 29. Claiborne County, with Tazewell as its seat, was created. It was named for William Charles Coles Claiborne, first governor of the Louisiana Territory, member of the Tennessee state constitutional convention and United States Representative from Tennessee.

November 6. Anderson, Jackson and Roane Counties were established. Anderson, with its seat at Clinton, was named for Joseph Anderson, United States Senator from Tennessee and the first comptroller of the United States Treasury.

Jackson, with Gainesboro as its seat, was named for Andrew Jackson, member of the Tennessee constitutional convention, United States Representative and Senator from Tennessee, and later seventh President of the United States.

Roane, with Kingston as its seat, was named for Archibald Roane, member of the Tennessee constitutional convention and second governor of the state.

1803   September 23. John Sevier, Democrat-Republican, became governor of the state. He served in the office until September 20, 1809.

October 25. Dickson and Rutherford Counties were established. Dickson, with its seat at Charlotte, was named for William Dickson, member of the state house of representatives and United States Representative from Tennessee.

Rutherford, with Murfreesboro as its seat, was named for Griffith Rutherford, who fought in the Revolutionary War, was a member of the North Carolina Senate and president of the Tennessee legislative council.

CHRONOLOGY 7

November 1. Stewart County was established, with its seat at Dover. It was named for Duncan Stewart.

1804   July 27. The state legislature ratified the 12th Amendment to the United States Constitution.

1806   September 11. Campbell, Overton, and White Counties were created. Campbell, with Jacksboro as its seat, was named for George Washington Campbell, United States Representative and Senator from Tennessee, United States Secretary of the Treasury in the Cabinet of President James Madison, and United States Minister to Russia.

Overton, with its seat at Livingston, was named for John Overton who founded Memphis and was a justice of the Tennessee Supreme Court.

White, with Sparta as its seat, was named for John White who fought in the Revolutionary War.

1807   November 16. Maury County, with its seat at Columbia, was established. It was named for Abram Maury.

November 26. Warren County, with its seat at McMinnville, was created. It was named for Joseph Warren, a physician who served as major general of the Continental Army and was killed at the battle of Bunker Hill on June 17, 1775.

November 30. Bledsoe and Rhea Counties were established. Bledsoe, with Pikeville as its seat, was named for Abraham Bledsoe who fought in the Revolutionary War and later in the War of 1812.

Rhea, with its seat at Dayton, was named for John Rhea who served in the Revolutionary War, was a member of the Tennessee House of Representatives, and was United States Representative from Tennessee.

December 30. Bedford and Franklin Counties were created. Bedford, with Shelbyville as its seat, was named for Captain Bedford, captain of H Company.

Franklin, with its seat at Winchester, was named for Benjamin Franklin, American official, member of the Continental Congress, signer of the Declaration of Independence, and member of the Constitutional Convention.

1809   September 20. Willie Blount, Democrat-Republican, became governor of Tennessee. He served in the office until September 27, 1815.

October 19. Humphreys County, with Waverly as its seat, was established. It was named for Parry Wayne Humphreys, a judge of the Tennessee courst and later United States Representative from the state.

November 14. Giles and Lincoln Counties were created. Giles, with Pulaski as its seat, was named for William Branch Giles, 25th governor of Virginia and member of the Virginia legislature.

Lincoln was named for Benjamin Lincoln, a major general in the Continental Army and Secretary of War for the Continental Congress. Its seat is at Fayetteville.

1810   Population: 261,727

1813   The first public library in the state was opened at Nashville.

1814   February 9. George W. Campbell became Secretary of the Treasury in the Cabinet of President James Madison.

1815   September 27. Joseph McMinn, Democrat-Republican, became governor of the state. He served in the office until October 1, 1821.

1817   October 15. Morgan County, with Wartburg as its seat, was created. It was named for Daniel Morgan, who served in the Revolutionary War, helped to suppress the Whiskey Rebellion in Pennsylvania and was United States Representative from Virginia.

October 21. Lawrence County, with its seat at Lawrenceburg, was established. It was named for James Lawrence, naval commander who fought in the war with Tripoli and issued the famous order "Don't give up the ship."

November 20. Marion County, with Jasper as its seat, was created. It was named for Francis Marion, brigadier general in the Revolutionary War who won the battle of Eutaw Springs and served in the South Carolina Senate.

November 24. Wayne County, with its seat at Waynesboro, was created. It was named for General Anthony Wayne who fought in the Revolutionary War, was major general and general-in-chief of the United States Army and defeated the Indians at the battle of Fallen Timbers in 1793.

1818   October 19. General Andrew Jackson negotiated a treaty with the Chicaksaw Indians for the purchase of Western Tennessee.

1819   October 25. Hamilton County was established, with Chattanooga as its seat. It was named for Alexander Hamilton, member of the Continental Congress and the Continental Army and United States Secretary of the Treasury in the Cabinet of President George Washington.

November 13. Hardin and Monroe Counties were created. Hardin, with its seat at Savannah, was named for Joseph Hardin, member of the Continental Army, speaker of the territorial assembly, and member of the state house of representatives.

Monroe, with Madisonville as its seat, was named for James Monroe, governor of Virginia, member of the Continental Congress, United States Senator from Virginia, United States Secretary of State in the administration of President James Madison and fifth President of the United States.

November 24. Shelby County, with Memphis as its seat, was established. It was named for Isaac Shelby, who served in the Revolutionary War and the War of 1812, was governor of Kentucky and a member of the North Carolina legislature.

Maryville College was established at Maryville.

1820　　　　Population: 422,823.

Elihu Emree began publication of the <u>Emancipator</u> at Jonesboro.

1821　　　　October 1. William Carroll, Democrat-Republican, became governor of Tennessee. He served in the office until October 1, 1827.

November 7. Carroll, Henderson, Henry and Madison Counties were created. Carroll, with Huntingdon as its seat, was named for William Carroll, who served under Andrew Jackson at the battle of New Orleans and was governor of Tennessee.

Henderson, with its seat at Lexington, was named for James Henderson, colonel of the Tennessee Militia and quartermaster on General Andrew Jackson's staff during the War of 1812.

Henry, with Paris as its seat, was named for Patrick Henry, member of the Continental Congress and governor of Virginia.

Madison, with Jackson as its seat, was named for James Madison, United States Secretary of State in the administration of President Thomas Jefferson and fourth President of the United States.

November 14. Perry County, with Linden as its seat, was established. It was named for Oliver Hazard Perry who supervised the construction and equipping of a fleet of nine ships on Lake Erie and fought and won the battle of Lake Erie, later becoming a commodore in the United States Navy.

1823　　　　October 8. McNair County, with its seat at Selmer, was created. It was named for John McNair, judge of the United States District Court for Tennessee.

October 16. Dyer and Hardemann Counties were established. Dyer, with Dyersburg as its seat, was named for Richard Henry Dyer who served in the Natchez expedition, the Creek War, the battle of New Orleans and the Seminole Campaign of 1818.

Hardemann, with Bolivar as its seat, was named for Thomas Jones Hardemann, colonel of the Tennessee Militia in the War of 1812 and member of the Congress of the Texan Republic.

October 21. Gibson and Waekley Counties were created. Gibson, with Trenton and Humboldt as its seats, was named for John Gibson who served with General Andrew Jackson in the Natchez campaign of 1812-13.

Weakley, with its seat at Dresden, was named for Robert Weakley who served in the Revolutionary War, was United States Representative from Tennessee, a member of the Tennessee Senate and the constitutional convention of 1834.

October 24. Obion County was established, with Union City as its seat.

October 29. Tipton County, with its seat at Covington, was created. It was named for Jacob Tipton who served under General Arthur St. Clair and was killed in a battle with the Indians in 1791.

November 23. Haywood County, with its seat at Brownsville, was established. It was named for John Haywood, attorney general of North Carolina and supreme court judge of Tennessee.

November 28. Fontess County, with Jamestown as its seat, was created. It was named for James Fontess, speaker of the Tennessee House of Representatives.

1825   Union University was founded at Kackson.

1826   Frances Wright founded Nashoba near Memphis as a planned community. Blacks were to be trained and then sent to live in colonies in Africa. The community remained in operation until 1828. It was held to be a moral danger because of Miss Wright's views on free love.

1827   October 1. Samuel Houston, Democrat-Republican, became governor of the state. He served in the office until his resignation on April 16, 1829.

1829   March 9. John H. Eaton became Secretary of War in the Cabinet of President Andrew Jackson.

April 16. William Hall, speaker of the state senate, became acting governor of Tennessee upon the resignation of Governor Samuel Houston. Hall served in the post until October 1, 1829.

October 1. William Carroll, Democrat, became governor of the state. He served in the office until October 12, 1835.

1830   Population: 681,904.

The public school system was begun by the state legislature.

1834   The second state constitution was adopted.

1835   October 12. Newton Cannon, Anti-Jackson Democrat, became governor of Tennessee. He served in the office until October 14, 1839.

November 24. Lauderdale County, with its seat at Riple, was created. It was named for James Lauderdale who was killed at the battle of New Orleans.

December 19. Benton County, with Camden as its seat, was established, effective January 1, 1836 and organized February 7, 1836. It was named for Thomas Hart Benton, Senator and Representative from Missouri.

The state agreed to subscribe to one-third of the capital stock of companies which were organized to construct turnpikes, railways and other means of transportation.

1836   January 2. Johnson County, with its seat at Mountain City, was created. It was named for Cave Johnson, United States Representative from Tennessee and Postmaster General of the United States in the administration of President James Knox Polk.

January 8. Coffee County, with Manchester as its seat, was established. It was named for John Coffee, colonel of the Tennessee volunteers, brigadier general of the Tennessee Mounted, leader of the Tennesseans at the battle of New Orleans and United States surveyor of public lands.

January 20. Meigs County was created, with Decatur as its seat. It was named for Return Jonathan Meigs, United States Senator from and governor of Ohio and Postmaster General in the administration of Presidents James Madison and James Monroe.

January 31. Cannon County, with its seat at Woodbury, was established. It was named for Newton Cannon, United States Representative from and governor of Tennessee.

February 10. Bradley County, with Cleveland as its seat, was created. It was named for Edward Bradley, lieutenant colonel of the first regiment of the Tennessee volunteers who fought in the Creek War.

February 20. Marshall County, with Lewisburg as its seat, was established. It was named for John Marshall, United States Secretary of State in the Cabinet of President John Adams and Chief Justice of the United States Supreme Court.

1837   December 11. De Kalb County was created, with its seat at Smithville. It was named for Johann De Kalb who served in the French Army, was commissioned major general in the Cintinental Army and died from wounds received at the Battle of Camden.

The southern boundary of the state was finally established at $35°$ latitude.

1838   July 5. Felix Grundy became Postmaster General of the United States in the administration of President Martin Van Buren.

The Cherokee Indians were forced to leave Tennessee.

The Bank of Tennessee was organized.

1839	October 14. James K. Polk, Democrat, became governor of the state. He served in the office until October 15, 1841. He was later eleventh President of the United States.

November 28. Polk County, with its seat at Benton, was created. It was named for James Knox Polk, United States Representative from Tennessee, governor of the state and later eleventh President of the United States. |
| 1840 | Population: 829,210.

January 3. Van Buren County, with Spencer as its seat, was established. It was named for Martin Van Buren, United States Senator from and governor of New York, Vice President of the United States under President Andrew Jackson and eighth President of the United States. |
| 1841 | March 5. John Bell became United States Secretary of War in the Cabinet of President William Henry Harrison.

October 15. James C. Jones, Whig, became governor of Tennessee. He remained in the office until October 14, 1845. |
| 1842 | January 18. Macon County, with its seat at LaFayette, was created. It was named for Nathaniel Macon, Revolutionary War veteran, United States Representative from North Carolina, Speaker of the United States House of Representatives, and United States Senator from North Carolina.

February 2. Putnam County was established, with Cookeville as its seat. It was named for Israel Putnam, who served in the French and Indian and Pontiac's Wars and was a major general in the Continental Army during the Revolutionary War.

Bethel College at McKenzie and Cumberland University at Lebanon were founded. |
| 1843 | December 21. Lewis County, with Hohenwald as its seat, was created. It was named for Meriwether Lewis, private secretary to President Thomas Jefferson, who led an expedition to the West with William Clark. |

Lewis was also governor of Louisiana Territory.

December 30. Cumberland University received its charter in Lebanon. It granted the first degrees in 1843.

Nashville was chosen as the permanent capital of the state.

Lambuth College was founded at Jackson.

1844   January 7. Hancock County, with its seat at Sneedville, was created. It was named for John Hancock, first governor of Massachusetts, president of the Continental Congress and first signer of the Declaration of Independence.

January 29. Grundy County, with Altamont as its seat, was established. It was named for Felix Grundy, United States Representative and Senator from Tennessee and Attorney General of the United States in the Cabinet of President Martin Van Buren.

March 6. Cave Johnson became Postmaster General of the United States in the Cabinet of President James Knox Polk.

October 14. Aaron V. Brown, Democrat, became governor of the state. He served in the office until October 17, 1847.

November. Decatur County, with its seat at Decaturville, was created. It was named for Stephen Decatur, member of the United States Navy who fought in the Tripolitan War and the War of 1812.

December 20. Crockett County was established, with its seat at Alamo. It became effective March 14, 1846 and was named for David Crockett, United States Representative from Tennessee, who aided Texan independence and died while defending the Alamo on March 6, 1836.

1847   October 17. Neill S. Brown, Whig, became governor of Tennessee. He served in the office until October 16, 1849.

1848   Burritt College at Spencer, Southwestern

University at Memphis, and the University of Tennessee were founded.

1849 October 16. William Trousdale, Democrat, became governor of Tennessee. He served in the office until October 16, 1851.

December 17. Scott County, with Huntsville as its seat, was created. It was named for Winfield Scott who served in the United States Army, fought in the War of 1812 and eventually became commander-in-cnief of the Army.

Hiawassee College was organized at Sweetwater.

1850 Population: 1,002,717.

June 3. A convention of slave state delegates met at Nashville. The respresentatives passed a resolution on June 10 calling for extension of the Missouri Compromise line to the Pacific Ocean.

Bethel College was established at McKenzie.

October 16. William B. Campbell, Whig, became governor of Tennessee. He served in the office until October 17, 1853.

Carson-Newman College was founded at Jefferson City.

1853 October 17. Andrew Johnson, Democrat, became governor of Tennessee. He served in the office until November 3, 1857. Johnson later became Vice President of the United States under President Abraham Lincoln and the 17th President of the United States.

1854 The state's first railroad was completed between Nashville and Chattanooga.

Christian Brothers College was founded at Memphis.

1855 November 16. Cumberland County was established, with its seat at Crossville. It was named for William Augustus, Duke of Cumberland, second son of King George II and Queen Caroline of England.

1856	February 28. Cheatham County, with Ashland City as its seat, was created. It was named for Edwin S. Cheatham, speaker of the Tennessee Senate at the time of the organization of the county.
1857	March 27. Memphis and Charleston Railroad was completed from the Atlantic Ocean to the Mississippi River. November 3. Isham G. Harris, Democrat, became governor of the state. He was forced to leave Nashville on March 12, 1862, because of the invasion of Union troops. December 9. Sequatchie County was established, with its seat at Dunlap. Tennessee Wesleyan College was organized at Athens.
1858	January 6. The University of the South received its charter at Sewanee. It awarded its first degrees in 1873.
1860	Population: 1,109,801.
1861	February 9. A proposition to call a convention to vote on the issue of secession was defeated. May 7. The state legislature entered into a military league with the Confederacy. June 8. The citizens of Tennessee voted in favor of secession. June 17. Representatives of all the eastern and several middle counties met in a convention. They petitioned the United States Congress to be admitted to the Union as a separate state. The request was ignored. June 24. Governor Isham G. Harris issued a proclamation declaring the state out of the Union.
1862	February. General Ulysses S. Grant and Commodore A. H. Foote captured Fort Henry on the Tennessee River and Fort Donelson on the Cumberland River.

March 12. Andrew Johnson became military governor of the state in which capacity he served until March 4, 1865.

April 6-7. General Ulysses S. Grant defeated southern troops in the Battle of Shiloh or Pittsburgh Landing.

April 7. Island No. 10 in the Mississippi River was captured by Union forces. The river was opened as far south as Memphis.

June. Memphis was captured.

December 31 - January 2, 1863. United States General William S. Rosencrans fought against Confederate General Braxton Bragg in the indecisive battle of Stone River or Murfreesboro.

1863
June. General William S. Rosencrans forced General Braxton Bragg out of Chattanooga.

September 19-20. The Battle of Chickamauga was fought.

November 23-25. General Ulysses S. Grant and his troops defeated Confederate troops at Chattanoga.

1864
April 12. Major General Forrest led Confederate troops in capturing Fort Pillow on the Mississippi River.

December 15-16. General Thomas led his Union troops against General J. B. Hood.

1865
March 4. Andrew Johnson was inaugurated as Vice President of the United States under President Abraham Lincoln.

April 5. William G. Brownlow, Republican, became governor of the state. He served in the office until his resignation on October 11, 1867.

April 7. The state legislature ratified the 13th Amendment to the United States Constitution.

December 24. The Ku Klux Klan was organized in the law office of Thomas M. Jones in Pulaski.

Fisk University was established in Nashville.

1866
April 2. President Andrew Johnson proclaimed the insurrection over in Tennessee.

July 19. The state legislature ratified the 14th Amendment to the United States Constitution.

July 24. Tennessee became the first Confederate state to be readmitted to the Union.

Walden University was founded at Nashville.

1867
May. The Ku Klux Klan which had been formed by Confederate officers as a social club was formally organized at Nashville.

October 11. Dewitt Clinton Senter, speaker of the state senate, a Conservative Republican, became governor of the state upon the resignation of Governor William G. Brownlow. Senter was subsequently elected to the post until October 10, 1871.

Blacks were given the right to vote by the state legislature.

King College at Bristol, Milligan College at Milligan and the University of Chattanooga were founded.

1868
The University of the South was established at Sewanee.

1870
Population: 1,258,520.

June 2. Loudon County, with Loudon as its seat, was established. It was named for John Campbell, fourth Earl of Loudon, commander-in-chief of the British forces in America. It was formerly called Christiana County and was changed to July 7, 1870.

June 8. Hamblen County, with Morristown as its seat, was created. It was named for Hezekiah Hamblen.

June 21. Trousdale County, with Hartsville as its seat, was established. It was named for William Trousdale who fought in the

War of 1812, was a member of the Tennessee legislature and was governor of the state.

June 24. Clay and Lake Counties were created. Clay, with Celina as its seat, was named for Henry Clay, United States Representative and Senator from Tennessee and United States Secretary of State in the administration of President John Quincy Adams.

Lake County has its seat at Tiptonville.

December 16. Bishop Paine founded the Colored Methodist Episcopal Church of America at Jackson.

A new state constitution was adopted, granting all male citizens over the age of 21 the right to vote.

Lemoyne-Owen College was founded at Memphis.

1871   January 23. Houston County, with Erin as its seat, was established. It was named for Samuel Houston, United States Representative from and governor of Tennessee, president of the Republic of Texas and governor of and United States Senator from Texas.

October 10. John C. Brown, Democrat, became governor of the state. He served in the office until January 18, 1875.

December 14. Moore County, with Lynchburg as its seat, was created. It was named for William Moore, major general in the War of 1812 and member of the Tennessee House of Representatives.

Christian Brothers College was organized at Memphis.

1872   Vanderbilt University was founded at Nashville.

1875   January 18. James D. Porter, Jr., Democrat, became governor of the state. He served in the office until February 16, 1879.

March 23. Unicoi County was established, with its seat at Erwin.

George Peabody College for Teachers was founded at Nashville. Knoxville College was organized.

1876   Meharry Medical College was founded in Nashville.

1877   March 12. David M. Key became Postmaster General of the United States in the Cabinet of President Rutherford B. Hayes.

1878   A yellow fever epidemic broke out, killing 5,200 of the 19,600 people in Memphis.

1879   February 16. Albert S. Marks, Democrat, became governor of Tennessee. He served in the office until January 17, 1881.

February 27. Rickett County, with Byrdstown as its seat, was created. It was named for H. L. Rickett, a representative from Wilson County who was instrumental in aiding in the establishment of the county.

March 4. Chester County, with its seat at Henderson, was established. It was named for Robert I. Chester, postmaster of Jackson and quartermaster of the Fourth Tennessee Regiment in the War of 1812.

1880   Population: 1,542,359.

June 2. Horace Maynard was appointed Postmaster General of the United States by President Rutherford B. Hayes. Maynard assumed his office as a member of the Cabinet on August 25, 1880.

1881   January 17. Alvin Hawkins, Republican, who had been elected in 1880, became governor of the state. He served in the office until January 15, 1883.

Milligan College was established at Milligan.

1882   Lane College was founded at Jackson.

1883	January 15. William B. Bate, Lowtax Democrat, who had been elected in 1882, became governor of Tennessee. He served in the office until January 17, 1887.
1885	South-western Presbyterian College was organized at Clarkville.
1887	January 17. Robert L. Taylor, Democrat, who had been elected in 1886, became governor of the state. He served in the post until January 19, 1891.
1890	Population: 1,767,518.
1891	January 19. John P. Buchanan, Democrat, who had been elected in 1890, became governor of the state. He served in the office until January 16, 1893.
1892	Scarritt College for Christian Workers at Nashville and Southern Missionary College at Collegedale were founded.
1893	January 16. Peter Turney, Democrat, who had been elected in 1892, became governor of Tennessee. He was reelected after a recount in 1894 and served in the office until January 21, 1897.
1897	January 21. Robert L. Taylor, Democrat, whp had been elected in 1896, became governor of Tennessee. He served in the office until January 16, 1899. Lincoln Memorial University was established at Harrogate.
1899	January 16. Banton McMillin, Democrat, who had been elected in 1898, became governor of the state. He was reelected in 1900 and served in the office until January 19, 1903.
1900	Population: 2,020,616.
1903	January 19. James B. Franzier, Democrat, who had been elected in 1902, became governor of Tennessee. He was reelected in 1904 and served in the post until his resignation on March 21, 1905 in order to enter the United States Senate.

1905	March 21. John I. Cox, speaker of the state senate, a Democrat, became governor of the state upon the resignation of Governor James B. Franzier. Cox served in the office until the end of the term on January 17, 1907.
1907	January 17. Malcolm R. Patterson, Democrat, who had been elected in 1906, became governor of the state. He served in the office until January 26, 1911.
1908	June 29. Luke E. Wright was appointed United States Secretary of War by President Theodore Roosevelt. Wright assumed his office as a member of the cabinet on July 1, 1908.
1909	March 5. Jacob M. Dickinson was appointed United States Secretary of War by President William Howard Taft. Dickinson assumed his office as a member of the cabinet on March 12, 1909.
	Tennessee adopted Prohibition.
	East Tennessee State University was founded at Johnson City.
1910	Population: 2,184,789.
1911	January 26. Ben W. Hooper, Republican, who had been elected in 1910, became governor of the state. He was reelected in 1912 and served in the post until January 17, 1915.
	April 7. The state legislature ratified the 16th Amendment to the United States Constitution.
	Middle Tennessee State University was organized at Murfreesboro.
1912	Tennessee State University was founded at Nashville.
1913	March 5. James Clark McReynolds was appointed Attorney General of the United States by President Woodrow Wilson. McReynolds assumed his office as a member of the cabinet on March 6.

April 1. The state legislature ratified the 17th Amendment to the United States Constitution.

The state legislature authorized the county governments to issue bonds for the construction of highways.

1915   January 17. Thomas C. Rye, Democrat, who had been elected in 1914, became governor of the state. He was reelected in 1916 and served until January 15, 1919.

Memphis State University and Tennessee Technological University at Cookeville were founded.

1919   January 13. The state legislature ratified the 18th Amendment to the United States Constitution.

January 15. Albert H. Roberts, Democrat, who had been elected in 1918, became governor of Tennessee. He served in the post until January 15, 1921.

1920   Population: 2,337,885.

August 18. The state legislature ratified the 19th Amendment to the United States Constitution.

1921   January 15. Alfred A. Taylor, Republican, who had been elected in 1920, became governor of the state. He remained in the office until January 16, 1923.

1922   The first radio station in the state, WNAV, opened at Knoxville.

1923   January 16. Austin Peay, Democrat, who had been elected in 1922, became governor of Tennessee. He was reelected in 1924 and 1926, serving in the post until his death on October 2, 1927.

1924   March 18. One of the worst tornadoes in the history of the nation up to this point destroyed several towns in the state.

1925   May 5. John Scopes, a teacher, was arrested in Dayton for having violated the state law forbidding the teaching of the theory of evolution.

July 10-21. The Scopes "monkey" trial was held in Dayton. John Scopes was defended by Clarence Darrow and Dudley Field Malone. William Jennings Bryan served as one of the prosecuting attorneys. Scopes was convicted of having violated the state law forbidding the teaching of evolution and was fined $100.00

July 20. William Jennings appeared on the stand of the Scopes trial in Dayton to answer Clarence Darrow's questions in regard to the Fundamentalist religious doctrine. Bryan was humiliated in his viewpoints concerning a strict reading of the Bible.

July 26. William Jennings Bryan died in the midst of the celebration of the state's victory in the Scopes "monkey" trial.

1926 Great Smoky Mountain National Park in North Carolina and Tennessee was created with 517,014 acres.

1927 October 3. Henry H. Horton, speaker of the state senate, a Democrat, became governor of Tennessee upon the death of Governor Austin Peay. Horton was subsequently elected and served in the office until January 17, 1933.

Austin Peay State University was established at Clarksville.

1930 Population: 2,616,556.

Bryan College was founded at Dayton.

1932 The Southern College of Optmetry was organized at Memphis.

1933 January 17. Hill McAllister, who had been elected in 1932, became governor of the state. He was reelected in 1934 and served in the post until January 15, 1937.

January 20. The state legislature ratified the 20th Amendment to the United States Constitution.

March 4. Cordell Hull became United States Secretary of State in the Cabinet of President Franklin D. Roosevelt.

May 18. The United States Congress passed the Tennessee Valley Act which created the Tennessee Valley Authority. It was intended to provide flood control for the Tennessee River and develop rural electrification.

August 11. The state legislature ratified the 21st Amendment to the United States Constitution.

1937   January 15. Gordon Browning, Democrat, who had been elected in 1936, became governor of the state. He served in the office until January 16, 1939.

1939   January 16. Prentice Cooper, Democrat, who had been elected in 1938, became governor of Tennessee. He was reelected in 1940 and 1942, remaining in the post until January 16, 1945.

1940   Population: 2,915,841.

The Memphis Academy of Arts was organized.

1942   The United States program for creation of an atomic bomb, the Manhattan Project, was constructed at Oak Ridge.

Trevacca Nazarene College was founded at Nashville.

1945   January 16. Tim Nance McCord, Democrat, who had been elected in 1944, became governor of the state. He was reelected in 1946 and served in the post until January 17, 1949.

David Lipscomb College was founded in Nashville.

1948   The first television station in the state began broadcasting at Memphis, WMCT-TV.

1949   January 17. Gordon Browning, Democrat, who had been elected in 1948, became governor of the state. He was reelected in 1950 and served in the office until January 15, 1953.

CHRONOLOGY 27

1950   Population: 3,291,718.

1951   February 20. The state legislature ratified the 22nd Amendment to the United States Constitution.

Belmont College was founded at Nashville.

1953   January 15. Frank G. Clement, Democrat, who had been elected in 1952, became governor of Tennessee. He was reelected in 1954 and served in the office until January 19, 1959.

November 3. Residents of the state voted their approval of the eight amendments to the state constitution which had been proposed by the first state constitutional convention since 1870. The term of the governor was lengthened from two to four years. No individual could serve two successive terms.

1955   Covenant College was organized at Lookout Mountain.

1956   April 2-3. Serious tornadoes caused much damage in Tennessee.

October 5. The state supreme court ruled that Tennessee's school segregation law was unconstitutional.

1959   January 19. Bufford Ellington, Democrat, who had been elected in 1958, became governor of the state. He served in the post until January 15, 1963.

1960   Population: 3,567,089.

1961   March 6. The state legislature ratified the 23rd Amendment to the United States Constitution.

1962   March 20. The United States Supreme Court ruled in a Tennessee case that the federal courts had a right and duty to try cases involving the distribution of state legislative seats.

1963   January 15. Frank G. Clemen, Democrat, who had been elected in 1962, became governor of the state. He served in the gubernatorial office until January 16, 1967.

March 21. The state legislature ratified the 24th Amendment to the United States Constitution.

September. Schools continued to have prayers in spite of the Supreme Court ruling to the contrary on June 17.

1964 November. Residents of the state approved the convening of a constitutional convention in 1965 to deal with the issue of reapportionment.

The Tennessee Space Institute was formed at Tullahoma.

1965 May 28. Governor Frank G. Clement signed some bills for Congressional redistricting and legislative reapportionment which had been passed on May 27.

1966 November. Howard H. Baker, Jr., became the first popularly elected Republican Senator from Tennessee.

1967 January 12. The state legislature ratified the 25th Amendment to the United States Constitution.

January 16. Buford Ellington, Democrat, who had been elected in 1966, again became governor of Tennessee. He served in the office until January 16, 1971.

1968 April 4. Black Civil Rights leader Martin Luther King, Jr., was assassinated at Memphis.

Lee College was founded at Cleveland.

1970 Population: 3,923,687.

1971 January 16. Winfield Dunn, Republican, who had been elected in 1970, became governor of the state. He served in the office until January 18, 1975.

March 23. The state legislature ratified the 26th Amendment to the United States Constitution.

1972 January 14. Atomic Energy Commission Chairman James R. Schlesinger announced the intention of the Tennessee Valley Authority and the Commonwealth Edison Company of Chicago to construct a breeder nuclear power plant in Tennessee.

The state legislature ratified the Equal Rights Amendment to the United States Constitution.

1974   April 23. The state legislature became the second legislature to try to rescind its ratification of the Equal Rights Amendment to the United States Constitution.

1975   January 18. Ray Blanton, Democrat, who had been elected in 1974, became governor of the state.

August 20. United States District Court Judge Frank Gray, Jr. and the Tennessee Supreme Court ruled unconstitutional a Tennesseee law of 1973 which required biology texts to provide equal space for other scientific and religious theories of creation, including the biblical one.

October 7. President Gerald Ford attended a White House regional conference on domestic problems at Knoxville.

1976   July 12. President Gerald R. Ford signed a bill which included funds for a demonstration nuclear breeder reactor in the state.

October 1. Democratic Presidential nominee Jimmy Carter spoke in Nashville.

1977   April 11. Tennessee enacted a state death penalty law when the legislature overrode Governor Ray Blanton's veto of the bill.

August 16. Famous rock and roll singer Elvis Presley died in Nashville.

BIOGRAPHICAL DIRECTORY

The selected list of governors, United States Senators and Members of the House of Representatives for Tennessee, 1794-1977, includes all persons listed in the Chronology for whom basic biographical data was readily available. Older biographical sources are frequently in conflict on certain individuals, and in such cases the source most commonly cited by later authorities was preferred.

ALEXANDER, Adam Rankin
    Federalist
    b. Rockbridge County, Va.
    d. Jackson, Tenn.
    U. S. Representative, 1823-27

ALLEN, Robert
    Democrat
    b. Augusta County, Va., June 19, 1778
    d. Carthage, Tenn., August 19, 1844
    U. S. Representative, 1819-27

ANDERSON, Alexander Outlaw
    Democrat
    b. "Soldiers' Rest," Jefferson County, Tenn.,
        November 10, 1794
    d. Knoxville, Tenn., May 23, 1869
    U. S. Senator, 1840-41

ANDERSON, Joseph
    ----
    b. near Philadelphia, Pa., November 5, 1757
    d. Washington, D. C., April 17, 1837
    U. S. Senator, 1797-1815; President pro
        tempore, 1804-05

ANDERSON, Josiah McNair
    Whig
    b. near Pikeville, Tenn., November 29, 1807
    d. at Looneys Creek, near present town of
        Whitewell, Tenn., November 8, 1861
    U. S. Representative, 1849-51

ANDERSON, William Coleman
    Republican
    b. Tusculum, near Greenville, Tenn., July
        10, 1853
    d. Newport, Tenn., September 8, 1902
    U. S. Representative, 1895-97

ANDERSON, William Robert
    Democrat
    b. Bakerville, Tenn., June 17, 1921
    U. S. Representative, 1965-

ARNELL, Samuel Mayes
    Republican
    b. Zion settlement, near Columbia, Tenn.,
        May 3, 1833
    d. Johnson City, Tenn., July 20, 1903
    U. S. Representative, 1866-71

ARNOLD, Thomas Dickens

b. Spotsylvania County, Va., May 3, 1798
d. Jonesboro, Tenn., May 26, 1870
U. S. Representative, 1831-33, 1841-43

ASHE, John Baptista
Whig
b. Rocky Point, N. C., 1810
d. Galveston, Tex., December 29, 1857
U. S. Representative, 1843-45

ATKINS, John DeWitt Clinton
Democrat
b. near Marly's Chapel, Tenn., June 4, 1825
d. Paris, Tenn., June 2, 1908
U. S. Representative, 1857-59, 1873-83

ATKINSON, Richard Merrill
Democrat
b. Nashville, Tenn., February 6, 1894
d. Nashville, Tenn., April 29, 1947
U. S. Representative, 1937-39

AUSTIN, Richard Wilson
b. Decatur, Ala., August 26, 1857
d. Washington, D. C., April 20, 1919
U. S. Representative, 1909-19

AVERY, William Tecumseh
Democrat
b. Hardeman County, Tenn., November 11, 1819
d. by drowning in Ten Mile Bayou, Ark., May 22, 1880
U. S. Representative, 1857-61

BACHMAN, Nathan Lynn
Democrat
b. Chattanooga, Tenn., August 2, 1878
d. Washington, D. C., April 23, 1937
U. S. Senator, 1933-37

BAILEY, James Edmond
Democrat
b. Montgomery County, Tenn., August 15, 1822
d. Clarksville, Tenn., December 29, 1885
U. S. Senator, 1877-81

BAKER, Howard Henry
Republican
b. Somerset, Ky., January 12, 1902
d. Knoxville, Tenn., January 7, 1964
U. S. Representative, 1951-64

BAKER, Irene B.
    Republican
    b. Sevierville, Tenn., November 17, 1901
    U. S. Representative, 1964-65

BAKER, La Mar
    Republican
    b. December 19, 1915
    U. S. Representative, 1971-

BALLENTINE, John Goff
    Democrat
    b. Pulaski, Tenn., May 20, 1825
    d. Pulaski, Tenn., November 23, 1915
    U. S. Representative, 1883-87

BARROW, Washington
    Whig
    b. Davidson, Tenn., October 5, 1807
    d. St. Louis, Mo., October 19, 1866
    U. S. Representative, 1847-49

BASS, Ross
    Democrat
    b. on a farm in Giles County, near Pulaski,
        Tenn., March 17, 1918
    U. S. Representative, 1955-64
    U. S. Senator, 1964-67

BATE, William Brimage
    Democrat
    b. near Castalian Springs, Tenn., October 7, 1826
    d. Washington, D. C., March 9, 1905
    Governor of Tennessee, 1883-86
    U. S. Senator, 1887-1905

BELL, John
    Whig
    b. near Nashville, Tenn., February 15, 1797
    d. at his home on the banks of the Cumber-
        land River, near Cumberland Furnace,
        Tenn., September 10, 1869
    U. S. Representative, 1827-29 (Democrat),
        1829-41 (Whig); Speaker, 1834
    U. S. Secretary of War, 1841
    U. S. Senator, 1847-59

BERRY, George Leonard
    Democrat
    b. Lee Valley, Tenn., September 12, 1882
    d. Pressmen's Home, Tenn., December 4, 1948
    U. S. Senator, 1937-38

BLACKWELL, Julius W.
　Van Buren Democrat
　b. Virginia
　d. ----
　U. S. Representative, 1839-41, 1843-45

BLAIR, John
　Democrat
　b. Blairs Mill, near Jonesborough (now
　　　Jonesboro), Tenn., September 13, 1790
　d. Jonesboro, Tenn., July 8, 1863
　U. S. Representative, 1823-35

BLANTON, Leonard Ray
　Democrat
　b. on a farm in Hardin County, Tenn., April
　　　10, 1930
　U. S. Representative, 1967-

BLANTON, Ray
　Democrat
　Governor of Tennessee, 1975-

BLOUNT, William
　----
　b. near Windsor, N. C., March 26, 1749
　d. Knoxville, Tenn., March 21, 1800
　Member Continental Congress (Virginia),
　　　1782-83, 1786-87
　U. S. Senator, 1796-97

BLOUNT, William
　Democrat-Republican
　b. Bertie County, N. C., April 18, 1768
　d. Clarksville, Tenn., September 10, 1835
　Governor of Tennessee, 1809-15

BLOUNT, William Grainger
　Democrat
　b. near New Bern, N. C., 1784
　d. Paris, Tenn., May 21, 1827
　U. S. Representative, 1815-19

BOWEN, John Henry
　Democrat
　b. Washington County, Va., September 1780
　d. Gallatin, Tenn., September 25, 1822
　U. S. Representative, 1813-15

BRABSON, Reese Bowen
　Democrat
　b. Brabsons Ferry, near Knoxville, Tenn.,

September 16, 1817
d. Chattanooga, Tenn., August 16, 1863
U. S. Representative, 1859-61

BRIDGES, George Washington
   Unionist
   b. Charleston, Tenn., October 9, 1825
   d. Athens, Tenn., March 16, 1873
   U. S. Representative, 1863

BRIGHT, John Morgan
   Democrat
   b. Fayetteville, Tenn., January 20, 1817
   d. Fayetteville, N. C., October 3, 1911
   U. S. Representative, 1871-81

BROCK, William Emerson
   Democrat
   b. near Mocksville, N. C., March 14, 1872
   d. Chattanooga, Tenn., August 5, 1950
   U. S. Senator, 1929-31

BROCK, William Emerson III
   Republican
   b. Chattanooga, Tenn., November 23, 1930
   U. S. Representative, 1963-71
   U. S. Senator, 1971-

BROWN, Aaron Venable
   Democrat
   b. Brunswick County, Va., August 15, 1795
   d. Washington, D. C., March 8, 1859
   U. S. Representative, 1839-45
   Governor of Tennessee, 1845-47
   U. S. Postmaster General, 1857-59

BROWN, Foster Vincent
   Republican
   b. near Sparta, Tenn., December 24, 1852
   d. Chattanooga, Tenn., March 26, 1937
   U. S. Representative, 1895-97

BROWN, John Calvin
   Democrat/Liberal Republican
   b. Giles County, Tenn., January 6, 1827
   d. Red Boiling Springs, Tenn., August 17, 1889
   Governor of Tennessee, 1871-75

BROWN, Joseph Edgar
   Republican
   b. Jasper, Tenn., February 11, 1880
   d. Chattanooga, Tenn., June 13, 1939
   U. S. Representative, 1921-23

BROWN, Milton
    Whig
    b. Lebanon, Ohio, February 28, 1804
    d. Jackson, Tenn., May 15, 1883
    U. S. Representative, 1841-47

BROWN, Neill Smith
    Whig
    b. Pulaski, Tenn., April 18, 1810
    d. January 30, 1886
    Governor of Tennessee, 1847-49

BROWNING, Gordon
    Democrat
    b. near Atwood, Tenn., November 22, 1889
    U. S. Representative, 1923-35
    Governor of Tennessee, 1937-39, 1949-53

BROWNLOW, Wlter Preston
    Republican
    b. Abingdon, Va., March 27, 1851
    d. National Soldiers' Home, Johnson City,
        Tenn., July 8, 1910
    U. S. Representative, 1897-1910

BROWNLOW, William Gannaway
    Republican
    b. near Wytheville, Va., August 29, 1805
    d. Knoxville, Tenn., April 29, 1877
    Governor of Tennessee, 1865-68
    U. S. Senator, 1869-75

BRYAN, Henry H.
    ----
    b. Martin County, N. C.,
    d. Montgomery County, Tenn., May 7, 1835
    U. S. Representative, 1819-23

BUCHANAN, John P.
    Democrat
    b. Tennessee, 1847
    d. May 14, 1930
    Governor of Tennessee, 1891-93

BUGG, Robert Malone
    Whig
    b. Boydton, Va., January 20, 1805
    d. Lynnville, Tenn., February 18, 1887
    U. S. Representative, 1853-55

BUNCH, Samuel
    Whig
    b. Grainger County, Tenn., December 4, 1786

d. on his farm near Rutledge, Tenn.,
   September 5, 1849
U. S. Representative, 1833-37

BUTLER, Mounce Gore
   Democrat
   b. Gainesboro, Tenn., May 11, 1849
   d. Gainesboro, Tenn., February 13, 1917
   U. S. Representative, 1905-07

BUTLER, Roderick Random
   Republican
   b. Wytheville, Va., April 9, 1827
   d. Mountain City, Tenn., August 18, 1902
   U. S. Representative, 1867-75, 1887-89

BYRNS, Joseph Wellington
   Democrat
   b. near Cedar Hill, Tenn., July 20, 1869
   d. Washington, D. C., June 4, 1936
   U. S. Representative, 1909-36; Speaker,
      1935-36

BYRNS, Joseph Wellington, Jr.
   Democrat
   b. Nashville, Tenn., August 15, 1903
   U. S. Representative, 1939-51

CALDWELL, Andrew Jackson
   Democrat
   b. Montevallo, Ala., July 22, 1837
   d. Nashville, Tenn., November 22, 1906
   U. S. Representative, 1883-87

CALDWELL, Robert Porter
   Democrat
   b. Adair County, Ky., December 16, 1821
   d. Trenton, Tenn., March 12, 1885
   U. S. Representative, 1871-73

CALDWELL, William Parker
   Democrat
   b. Christmasville, Tenn., November 8, 1832
   d. Gardner, Tenn., June 7, 1903
   U. S. Representative, 1875-79

CAMPBELL, Brookins
   Democrat
   b. Washington County, Tenn., 1808
   d. Washington, D. C., December 25, 1853
   U. S. Representative, 1853

CAMPBELL, George Washington

Democrat
b. Parish of Tongue, Setterlandshire, Scotland, February 9, 1769
d. Nashville, Tenn., February 17, 1848
U. S. Representative, 1803-09
U. S. Senator, 1811-14
U. S. Secretary of the Treasury, 1814
U. S. Senator, 1815-18

CAMPBELL, William Bowen
Democrat
b. near Hendersonville, Tenn., February 1, 1807
d. near Lebanon, Tenn., August 19, 1867
U. S. Representative, 1837-43 (Whig)
Governor of Tennessee, 1851-53
U. S. Representative, 1866-67

CANNON, Newton
Whig
b. Guilford County, N. C., May 22, 1781
d. Harpeth, Tenn., September 16, 1841
Governor of Tennessee, 1835-39

CARMACK, Edward Ward
Democrat
b. near Castalian Springs, Tenn., November 5, 1858
d. Nashville, Tenn., November 9, 1908
U. S. Representative, 1897-1901
U. S. Senator, 1901-07

CARROLL, William
Democrat
b. Pittsburgh, Pa., March 3, 1788
d. Nashville, Tenn., March 22, 1844
Governor of Tennessee, 1821-27 (Democrat-Republican), 1829-35 (Democrat)

CARTER, William Blount
Whig
b. Elizabethton, Tenn., October 22, 1792
d. Elizabethton, Tenn., April 17, 1848
U. S. Representative, 1835-41

CARUTHERS, Robert Looney
Whig
b. Smith County, Tenn., July 31, 1800
d. Lebanon, Tenn., October 2, 1882
U. S. Representative, 1841-43

CHANDLER, Walter
Democrat

b. Jackson, Tenn., October 5, 1887
d. Memphis, Tenn., October 1, 1967
U. S. Representative, 1935-40

CHASE, Lucien Bonaparte
    Democrat
    b. Derby Line, Vt., December 5, 1817
    d. Derby Line, Vt., December 4, 1864
    U. S. Representative, 1845-49

CHEATHAM, Richard
    Whig
    b. Springfield, Tenn., February 20, 1799
    d. at White's Creek Springs, near Tennessee, September 9, 1845
    U. S. Representative, 1837-39

CHURCHWELL, William Montgomery
    Democrat
    b. near Knoxville, Tenn., February 20, 1826
    d. Knoxville, Tenn., August 18, 1862
    U. S. Representative, 1851-55

CLAIBORNE, Thomas
    Democrat
    b. near Petersburg, Va., May 17, 1780
    d. Nashville, Tenn., January 7, 1856
    U. S. Representative, 1817-19

CLAIBORNE, William Charles Coe
    b. Sussex County, Va., 1775
    d. New Orleans, La., November 23, 1817
    U. S. Representative, 1797-1801 (Tennessee)
    Governor (Territory of Mississippi), 1801-03
    Governor (Territory of Orleans), 1804-12
    Governor of Louisiana, 1812-16
    U. S. Senator, 1817 (Louisiana)

CLEMENT, Frank Good
    Democrat
    b. Dickson, Tenn., June 2, 1920
    d. November 4, 1969
    Governor of Tennessee, 1953-59, 1963-67

CLEMENTS, Andrew Jackson
    Unionist
    b. Clementsville, Tenn., December 23, 1832
    d. Glasgow, Ky., November 7, 1913
    U. S. Representative, 1861-63

CLOUSE, Wynne F.
    Republican
    b. Graffton, near Cookeville, Tenn., August

29, 1883
d. Franklin, Tenn., February 19, 1944
U. S. Representative, 1921-23

COCKE, John
----
b. Brunswick, Va., 1772
d. Rutledge, Tenn., February 16, 1854
U. S. Representative, 1819-27

COCKE, William
----
b. Amelia County, Tenn., 1747
d. Columbus, Miss., August 22, 1848
U. S. Senator, 1796-97, 1797, 1799-1805

COCKE, William Michael
Democrat
b. Rutledge, Tenn., July 16, 1815
d. Nashville, Tenn., February 6, 1896
U. S. Representative, 1845-49

COOPER, Edmund
Conservative
b. Franklin, Tenn., September 11, 1821
d. Shelbyville, Tenn., July 21, 1911
U. S. Representative, 1866-67

COOPER, Henry
Democrat
b. Columbia, Tenn., August 22, 1827
d. Tierra Blanca, Guadalupe y Calvo, Mexico, February 3, 1884
U. S. Senator, 1871-77

COOPER, Jere
Democrat
b. on a farm near Dyersburg, Tenn., July 20, 1893
d. at the naval hospital, Bethesda, Md., December 18, 1957
U. S. Representative, 1929-57

COOPER, Prentice
Democrat
b. Shelbyville, Tenn., September 8, 1895
d. May 18, 1969
Governor of Tennessee, 1939-45

COURTNEY, William Wirt
Democrat
b. Franklin, Tenn., September 7, 1889

      d. Franklin, Tenn., April 6, 1961
      U. S. Representative, 1939-49

COX, John I.
    Democrat
    Governor of Tennessee, 1905-07

COX, Nicholas Nichols
    Democrat
    b. Bedford County, Tenn., January 6, 1837
    d. Franklin, Tenn., May 2, 1912
    U. S. Representative, 1891-1901

CROCKETT, David
    Whig
    b. at the point where Limestone Creek and the Noli-Chuckey River meet in the state of Franklin, which became Greene County, Tenn., August 17, 1786
    d. defending the Alamo, San Antonio de Bexar, May 6, 1836
    U. S. Representative, 1827-31 (Democrat), 1833-35 (Whig)

CROCKETT, John Wesley
    Whig
    b. Trenton, Tenn., July 10, 1807
    d. Memphis, Tenn., November 24, 1852
    U. S. Representative, 1837-41

CROZIER, John Hervey
    Whig
    b. Knoxville, Tenn., February 10, 1812
    d. Knoxville, Tenn., October 25, 1889
    U. S. Representative, 1845-49

CRUMP, Edward Hull
    Democrat
    b. on a farm near Holly Springs, Miss., October 2, 1874
    d. Memphis, Tenn., October 16, 1954
    U. S. Representative, 1931-35

CRUTCHFIELD, William
    Republican
    b. Greenville, Tenn., November 16, 1824
    d. Chattanooga, Tenn., January 24, 1890
    U. S. Representative, 1873-75

CULLOM, Alvan
    Democrat
    b. Monticello, Ky., September 4, 1797
    d. Livingston, Tenn., July 20, 1877

U. S. Representative, 1843-47

CULLOM, William
    Whig
    b. near Monticello, Ky., June 4, 1810
    d. Clinton, Tenn., December 6, 1896
    U. S. Representative, 1851-55

DAVIS, Edwin Lamar
    Democrat
    b. Bedford County, Tenn., February 5, 1876
    d. Washington, D. C., October 23, 1949
    U. S. Representative, 1919-33

DESHA, Robert
    ----
    b. near Gallatin, Tenn., January 14, 1791
    d. Mobile, Ala., February 6, 1849
    U. S. Representative, 1827-31

DIBNELL, George Gibbs
    Democrat
    b. Sparta, Tenn., April 12, 1822
    d. Sparta, Tenn., May 9, 1888
    U. S. Representative, 1875-85

DICKINSON, David W.
    Whig
    b. Franklin, Tenn., June 10, 1808
    d. at "Grantland," his father's home, near
        Murfreesboro, Tenn., April 27, 1845
    U. S. Representative, 1833-35 (Democrat),
        1843-45 (Whig)

DICKSON, William
    ----
    b. Duplin County, N. C., May 5, 1770
    d. Nashville, Tenn., February 1816
    U. S. Representative, 1801-07

DUNCAN, John James
    Republican
    b. Huntsville, Tenn., March 24, 1919
    U. S. Representative, 1965--

DUNLAP, William Claiborne
    Democrat
    b. Knoxville, Tenn., February 25, 1798
    d. near Memphis, Tenn., November 16, 1872
    U. S. Representative, 1833-37

DUNN, Winfield
    Republican

b. Meridian, Miss., July 1, 1927
Governor of Tennessee, 1971-75

EARTHMAN, Harold Henderson
  Democrat
  b. Murfreesboro, Tenn., April 13, 1900
  U. S. Representative, 1945-47

EATON, John Henry
  Democrat
  b. near Scotland Neck, N. C., June 18, 1790
  d. Washington, D. C., November 17, 1856
  U. S. Senator, 1818-21, 1821-29
  U. S. Secretary of War, 1829-31
  Governor (Florida Territory), 1834-36

ELLINGTON, Buford
  Democrat
  b. Holmes County, Miss., June 27, 1907
  d. April 3, 1972
  Governor of Tennessee, 1959-63, 1967-71

ENLOE, Benjamin Augustine
  Democrat
  b. near Clarksburg, Tenn., January 18, 1848
  d. Nashville, Tenn., July 8, 1922
  U. S. Representative, 1887-95

ESLICK, Edward Everett
  Democrat
  b. near Pulaski, Tenn., April 19, 1872
  d. Washington, D. C., June 14, 1932
  U. S. Representative, 1925-32

ESLICK, Willa McCord Blake
  Democrat
  b. Fayetteville, Tenn., September 8, 1878
  d. Pulaski, Tenn., February 18, 1961
  U. S. Representative, 1932-33

ETHERIDGE, Emerson
  Whig
  b. Currituck, N. C., September 28, 1819
  d. Dresden, Tenn., October 21, 1902
  U. S. Representative, 1853-57, 1859-61

EVANS, Henry Clay
  Republican
  b. Juniata County, Pa., June 18, 1843
  d. Chattanooga, Tenn., December 12, 1921
  U. S. Representative, 1889-91

EVERETT, Robert Ashton
    Democrat
    b. on a farm near Union City, Tenn., February 24, 1915
    d. Nashville, Tenn., January 26, 1969
    U. S. Representative, 1958-69

EVINS, Joseph Landon
    Democrat
    b. on a farm near Liberty, Tenn., October 24, 1910
    U. S. Representative, 1947-

EWING, Andrew
    Democrat
    b. Nashville, Tenn., June 17, 1813
    d. Atlanta, Ga., June 16, 1864
    U. S. Representative, 1849-51

EWING, Edwin Hickman
    Whig
    b. Nashville, Tenn., December 2, 1809
    d. Murfreesboro, Tenn., April 24, 1902
    U. S. Representative, 1845-47

FISHER, Hubert Frederick
    Democrat
    b. Milton, Fla., October 6, 1877
    d. New York, N. Y., June 16, 1941
    U. S. Representative, 1917-31

FITE, Samuel McClary
    Democrat
    b. near Alexandria, Tenn., June 12, 1816
    d. Hot Springs, Ark., October 23, 1875
    U. S. Representative, 1875

FITZGERALD, William
    Jackson Democrat
    b. Port Tobacco, Md., August 6, 1799
    d. Paris, Tenn., March 1864
    U. S. Representative, 1831-33

FITZPATRICK, Morgan Cassius
    Democrat
    b. near Carthage, Tenn., October 29, 1868
    d. Nashville, Tenn., June 25, 1908
    U.S. Representative, 1903-05

FORESTER, John B.
    ----
    b. McMinnville, Tenn.
    d. August 31, 1845

U. S. Representative, 1833-37

FOSTER, Ephraim Hubbard
    Whig
    b. near Bardstown, Ky., September 17, 1794
    d. Nashville, Tenn., September 14, 1854
    U. S. Senator, 1838-39, 1843-45

FOWLER, Joseph Smith
    Union Republican
    b. Steubenville, Ohio, August 31, 1820
    d. Washington, D. C., April 1, 1902
    U. S. Senator, 1866-71

FRAZIER, James Beriah
    Democrat
    b. Pikeville, Tenn., October 18, 1856
    d. Chattanooga, Tenn., March 28, 1937
    Governor of Tennessee, 1902-05
    U. S. Senator, 1905-11

FRAZIER, James Beriah, Jr.
    Democrat
    b. Chattanooga, Tenn., June 28, 1890
    U. S. Representative, 1949-63

FULTON, Richard Harmon
    Democrat
    b. Nashville, Tenn., January 27, 1927
    U. S. Representative, 1963-

GAINES, John Wrsley
    Democrat
    b. Wrencoe, near Nashville, Tenn., August 24, 1860
    d. Nashville, Tenn., July 4, 1926
    U. S. Representative, 1897-1909

GARRETT, Abraham Ellison
    Democrat
    b. near Livingston, Tenn., March 6, 1830
    d. Carthage, Tenn., February 14, 1907
    U. S. Representative, 1871-73

GARRETT, Finis James
    Democrat
    b. near Ore Springs, Tenn., August 26, 1875
    d. Washington, D. C., May 25, 1956
    U. S. Representative, 1905-29

GENTRY, Meredith Poindexter
    Whig
    b. Rockingham County, N. C., September 15, 1809

d. Nashville, Tenn., November 2, 1866
   U. S. Representative, 1839-43, 1845-53

GIBSON, Henry Richard
   Republican
   b. Kent Island, Md., December 24, 1837
   d. Washington, D. C., May 25, 1938
   U. S. Representative, 1895-1905

GLASS, Presley Thornton
   Democrat
   b. Houston, Va., October 18, 1824
   d. Ripley, Tenn., October 9, 1902
   U. S. Representative, 1885-89

GOLLADAY, Edward Isaac
   Democrat
   b. Lebanon, Tenn., September 9, 1830
   d. Columbia, S. C., July 11, 1897
   U. S. Representative, 1871-73

GORDON, George Washington
   Democrat
   b. Pulaski, Tenn., October 5, 1836
   d. Memphis, Tenn., August 9, 1911
   U. S. Representative, 1907-11

GORE, Albert Arnold
   Democrat
   b. Granville, Tenn., December 26, 1907
   U. S. Representative, 1939-44, 1945-53
   U. S. Senator, 1953-71

GRIDER, George William
   Democrat
   b. Memphis, Tenn., October 1, 1912
   U. S. Representative, 1965-67

GRUNDY, Felix
   War Democrat
   b. Berkely County, Tenn., September 11, 1777
   d. Nashville, Tenn., December 19, 1840
   U. S. Representative, 1811-14
   U. S. Senator, 1829-38
   U. S. Attorney General, 1838-39
   U. S. Senator, 1839-40

HALL, William
   Democrat
   b. Durry County, N. C., February 11, 1775
   d. on his farm "Locust Land," near Cas-
      talian Springs, Tenn., October 7, 1856
   Governor of Tennessee, 1829

U. S. Representative, 1831-33

HARRIS, Isham Green
Democrat
b. near Tullahoma, Tenn., February 10, 1818
d. Washington, D. C., July 8, 1897
U. S. Representative, 1849-53
Governor of Tennessee, 1858-64
U. S. Senator, 1877-97; President pro tempore, 1893-95

HARRIS, Thomas K.
Democrat
b. ----
d. from wounds received in an encounter with Col. John W. Simpson on the old Kentucky Road at Shells Ford between Sparta and McMinnville, Tenn., March 18, 1816
U. S. Representative, 1813-15

HARRISON, Horace Harrison
Republican
b. Lebanon, Tenn., August 7, 1829
d. Nashville, Tenn., December 20, 1885
U. S. Representative, 1873-75

HASKELL, William T.
Whig
b. Murfreesboro, Tenn., July 21, 1818
d. Hopkinsville, Ky., March 12, 1859
U. S. Representative, 1847-49

HATTON, Robert Hopkins
American Party
b. Steubenville, Ohio, November 2, 1826
d. at the battle of Seven Pines, near Richmond, Va., May 31, 1862

HAWKINS, Alvin
Republican
b. Bath County, Ky., December 2, 1821
d. 1905
Governor of Tennessee, 1881-83

HAWKINS, Isaac Roberts
Republican
b. near Columbia, Tenn., May 16, 1818
d. Huntingdon, Tenn., August 12, 1880
U. S. Representative, 1866-71

HENDERSON, Bennett H.
----
    b. Bedford, Va., September 5, 1784
    d. Summitville, Tenn.
    U. S. Representative, 1815-17

HILL, Hugh Lawson White
    Democrat
    b. near McMinnville, Tenn., March 1, 1810
    d. Hills Creek, Tenn., January 18, 1892
    U. S. Representative, 1847-49

HOGG, Samuel
    Democrat
    b. Halifax, N. C., April 18, 1783
    d. Rutherford County, Tenn., May 28, 1842
    U. S. Representative, 1817-19

HOOPER, Ben W.
    Republican
    b. Newport, Tenn., October 13, 1870
    d. April 18, 1957
    Governor of Tennessee, 1911-15

HORTON, Henry Hollis
    Democrat
    b. Princeton, Ala., February 17, 1866
    d. July 2, 1934
    Governor of Tennessee, 1933-37

HOUK, John Chiles
    Republican
    b. Clinton, Tenn., February 26, 1860
    d. Fountain City, Tenn., June 3, 1923
    U. S. Representative, 1891-95

HOUK, Leonidas Campbell
    Republican
    b. near Boyds Creek, Tenn., June 8, 1836
    d. Knoxville, Tenn., May 25, 1891
    U. S. Representative, 1879-91

HOUSE, John Ford
    Democrat
    b. near Franklin, Tenn., January 9, 1827
    d. Clarksville, Tenn., June 28, 1904
    U. S. Representative, 1875-83

HOUSTON, Samuel
    Democrat (Tennessee/Texas)
    b. Timber Ridge Church, near Lexington,
        Va., March 2, 1793
    d. Huntsville, Texas, July 26, 1863

U. S. Representative, 1823-27 (Tennessee)
Governor of Tennessee, 1827-29
U. S. Senator, 1846-59 (Texas)
Governor of Texas, 1859-61

HOUSTON, William Cannon
    Democrat
    b. near Shelbyville, Tenn., March 17, 1852
    d. on his plantation "Beaver Dam," near Woodbury, Tenn., August 30, 1931
    U. S. Representative, 1905-19

HULL, Cordell
    Democrat
    b. Olympus County, Tenn., October 2, 1871
    d. Bethesda, Md., July 23, 1955
    U. S. Representative, 1907-21, 1923-31
    U. S. Senator, 1931-33
    U. S. Secretary of State, 1933-44

HUMPHREYS, Parry Wayne
    Democrat
    b. Staunton, Va., 1778
    d. Hernando, Miss., February 12, 1839
    U. S. Representative, 1813-15

HUNTSMAN, Adam
    Jackson Democrat
    b. Virginia
    d. ----
    U. S. Representative, 1835-37

INGE, William Marshall
    Democrat
    b. Granville County, N. C., 1802
    d. Livingston, Ala., 1846
    U. S. Representative, 1833-35

ISACKS, Jacob C.
    ----
    b. Montgomery County, Pa.
    d. Winchester, Tenn.
    U. S. Representative, 1823-33

IZARD, Ralph
    ----
    b. Charleston, S. C., January 23, 1742
    d. Charleston, S. C., May 30, 1804
    Member Continental Congress, 1782-83
    U. S. Senator, 1789-95; President pro tempore, 1794-95

JACKSON, Andrew
    Democrat
    b. Waxhaw Settlement, S. C., March 15, 1767
    d. Nashville, Tenn., June 8, 1845
    U. S. Representative, 1796-97
    U. S. Senator, 1797-98
    Governor of Florida, 1821
    U. S. Senator, 1823-25
    7th President of the United States, 1829-37

JACKSON, Howell Edmunds
    Democrat
    b. Paris, Tenn., April 8, 1832
    d. West Meade, Tenn., August 8, 1895
    U. S. Senator, 1881-86
    Associate Justice of the U. S. Supreme
        Court, 1894-95

JARNAGIN, Spencer
    Whig
    b. Grainger County, Tenn., 1792
    d. Memphis, Tenn., June 25, 1853
    U. S. Senator, 1843-47

JENNINGS, John, Jr.
    Republican
    b. Jackson, Tenn., June 6, 1880
    d. Knoxville, Tenn., February 27, 1956
    U. S. Representative, 1939-51

JOHNSON, Andrew
    Republican
    b. Raleigh, N. C., December 29, 1808
    d. Elizabethton, Tenn., July 31, 1875
    U. S. Representative, 1843-53 (Democrat)
    Governor of Tennessee, 1853-57 (Democrat)
    Vice President of the United States, 1865
    17th President of the United States, 1865-69
    U. S. Senator, 1875 (Republican)

JOHNSON, Cave
    Democrat
    b. Robertson County, Tenn., January 11, 1795
    d. Clarksville, Tenn., November 23, 1866
    U. S. Representative, 1829-37, 1839-45
    U. S. Postmaster General, 1845-49

JONES, Ed
    Democrat
    b. Gibson County, Tenn., April 20, 1912
    U. S. Representative, 1969-

JONES, Francis
----
b. Tennessee
d. Winchester, Tenn.
U. S. Representative, 1817-23

JONES, George Washington
Democrat
b. King and Queen County, Va., March 15, 1806
d. Fayetteville, Tenn., November 14, 1884
U. S. Representative, 1843-59

JONES, James Chamberlain
Whig
b. on the line between Davidson and Wilson
   Counties, Tenn., April 20, 1809
d. Memphis, Tenn., October 29, 1859
Governor of Tennessee, 1841-45
U. S. Senator, 1851-57

KEFAUVER, Carey Estes
Democrat
b. on a farm near Madisonville, Tenn., July 26, 1903
d. Bethesda, Md., August 10, 1963
U. S. Representative, 1939-49
U. S. Senator, 1949-63

KEY, David McKendree
Democrat
b. near Greenville, Tenn., January 27, 1824
d. Chattanooga, Tenn., February 3, 1900
U. S. Senator, 1875-77
U. S. Postmaster General, 1877-80

KUYKENDALL, Dan Heflin
Republican
b. Cherokee, Tex., July 9, 1924
U. S. Representative, 1967-

LEA, Luke
Union Democrat
b. Surry County, N. C., January 21, 1783
d. Fort Leavenworth, Kansas, June 17, 1851
U. S. Representative, 1833-37

LEA, Luke
Democrat
b. Nashville, Tenn., April 12, 1879
d. Nashville, Tenn., November 18, 1945
U. S. Senator, 1911-17

LEA, Pryor
Jackson Democrat

b. Knox County, Tenn., August 31, 1794
d. Goliad, Texas, September 14, 1879
U. S. Representative, 1827-31

LEFTWICH, John William
Democrat
b. Liberty, Va., September 7, 1826
d. Huntsville, Ala., March 6, 1870
U. S. Representative, 1866-67

LEWIS, Barbour
Republican
b. Alburg, Vt., January 5, 1818
d. Colfax, Washington, July 15, 1893
U. S. Representative, 1873-75

LOSER, Joseph Carlton
Democrat
b. Nashville, Tenn., October 1, 1892
U. S. Representative, 1957-63

LOVETTE, Oscar Byrd
Republican
b. Greenville, Tenn., December 20, 1871
d. Granville, Tenn., July 6, 1934
U. S. Representative, 1931-33

MARABLE, John Hartwell
National Republican
b. near Lawrenceville, Va., November 18, 1786
d. Montgomery County, Tenn., April 11, 1844
U. S. Representative, 1825-29

MARKS, Albert S.
Democrat
Governor of Tennessee, 1887-91

MARR, George Washington Lent
----
b. near Marrs Hill, Va., May 25, 1779
d. at his residence on Island No. 10 in
   the Mississippi River, near New Madrid,
   Mo., September 5, 1856
U. S. Representative, 1817-19

MARTIN, Barclay
Democrat
b. Edgefield District, S. C., December 17, 1802
d. Columbia, Tenn., November 8, 1890
U. S. Representative, 1845-47

MASSEY, Zachary David

Republican
b. near Marshall, N. C., November 14, 1864
d. Sevierville, Tenn., July 13, 1923
U. S. Representative, 1910-11

MAURY, Abram Poindexter
Whig
b. near Franklin, Tenn., December 26, 1801
d. near Franklin, Tenn., July 22, 1848
U. S. Representative, 1835-39

MAYNARD, Horace
Republican
b. Westboro, Mass., August 30, 1814
d. Knoxville, Tenn., May 3, 1882
U. S. Representative, 1857-63 (American Party), 1866-75 (Republican)
U. S. Postmaster General, 1880-81

MCALISTER, Hill
Democrat
b. Nashville, Tenn., July 15, 1875
d. ----
Governor of Tennessee, 1933-37

MCCALL, John Ethridge
Republican
b. Clarksburg, Tenn., August 14, 1859
d. Huntingdon, Tenn., August 8, 1920
U. S. Representative, 1895-97

MCCLELLAN, Abraham
Democrat
b. "White Top," on Beaver Creek, Sullivan County, Tenn., October 4, 1789
d. "White Top," on Beaver Creek, Sillivan County, Tenn., May 3, 1866
U. S. Representative, 1837-43

MCCORD, James Nance
Democrat
b. Unionville, Tenn., March 17, 1879
d. Nashville, Tenn., September 2, 1968
U. S. Representative, 1943-45
Governor of Tennessee, 1945-49

MCDEARMON, James Calvin
Democrat
b. New Canton, Va., June 13, 1844
d. Trenton, Tenn., July 19, 1902
U. S. Representative, 1893-97

MCFARLAND, William
    Democrat
    b. Springvale Farm, near Morristown, Tenn.,
        September 15, 1821
    d. Morristown, Tenn., April 12, 1900
    U. S. Representative, 1875-77

MCKELLAR, Kenneth Douglas
    Democrat
    b. Richmond, Ala., January 29, 1869
    d. Memphis, Tenn., October 25, 1957
    U. S. Representative, 1911-17
    U. S. Senator, 1917-53; President pro
        tempore, 1945-47, 1949-53

MCMILLIN, Benton
    Democrat
    b. Monroe County, Ky., September 11, 1845
    d. Nashville, Tenn., January 8, 1933
    U. S. Representative, 1879-99
    Governor of Tennessee, 1899-1903

MCMINN, Joseph
    Democrat-Republican
    b. Marlborough Township, Pa., June 22, 1758
    d. Cherokee Agy, Tenn., November 17, 1824
    Governor of Tennessee, 1815-21

MCREYNOLDS, Samuel Davis
    Democrat
    b. Pikeville, Tenn., April 16, 1872
    d. Washington, D. C., July 11, 1939
    U. S. Representative, 1923-39

MILLER, Pleasant Moorman
    ----
    b. Lynchburg, Va.
    d. Tennessee, 1849
    U. S. Representative, 1809-11

MITCHELL, James Coffield
    ----
    b. Staunton, Va., March 1786
    d. near Jackson, Miss., August 7, 1843
    U. S. Representative, 1825-29

MITCHELL, John Ridley
    Democrat
    b. Livingston, Tenn., September 26, 1877
    d. Crossville, Tenn.
    U. S. Representative, 1931-39

MOON, John Austin

Democrat
b. near Charlottesville, Va., April 22, 1855
d. Chattanooga, Tenn., June 26, 1921
U. S. Representative, 1897-1921

MOORE, William Robert
Republican
b. Huntsville, Ala., March 28, 1830
d. Memphis, Tenn., June 12, 1909
U. S. Representative, 1881-83

MULLINS, James
Republican
b. Bedford County, Tenn., September 15, 1847
d. Shelbyville, Tenn., June 26, 1873
U. S. Representative, 1867-69

MURRAY, Thomas Jefferson
Democrat
b. Jackson, Tenn., August 1, 1894
U. S. Representative, 1943-66

NEAL, John Randolph
Democrat
b. Clinton, Tenn., November 26, 1836
d. Rhea Springs, Tenn., March 26, 1889
U. S. Representative, 1885-89

NELSON, Thomas Amos Rogers
Unionist
b. Kingston, Tenn., March 19, 1812
d. Knoxville, Tenn., August 24, 1873
U. S. Representative, 1859-61

NICHOLSON, Alfred Osborn Pope
Democrat
b. Franklin, Tenn., August 31, 1808
d. Washington, D. C., March 23, 1876
U. S. Senator, 1840-42, 1859-61

NUNN, David Alexander
Republican
b. Milton, N. H., July 26, 1833
d. Strafford County, N. H., September 11, 1918
U. S. Representative, 1867-69, 1873-75

PADGETT, Lemuel Phillips
Democrat
b. Columbia, Tenn., November 28, 1855
d. Washington, D. C., August 2, 1922
U. S. Representative, 1901-22

PATTERSON, David Trotter
   Democrat
   b. Cedar Creek, Tenn., February 28, 1818
   d. Afton, Tenn., November 3, 1891
   U. S. Senator, 1866-69

PATTERSON, Josiah
   Democrat
   b. Morgan County, Ala., April 14, 1837
   d. Memphis, Tenn., February 10, 1904
   U. S. Representative, 1891-97

PATTERSON, Malcolm Rice
   Democrat
   b. Somerville, Ala., June 7, 1861
   d. Sarasota, Fla., March 8, 1935
   U. S. Representative, 1901-06
   Governor of Tennessee, 1906-10

PEARSON, Herron Carney
   Democrat
   b. Taylor, Texas, July 31, 1890
   d. Jackson, Tenn., April 24, 1953
   U. S. Representative, 1935-43

PEAY, Austin
   Democrat
   b. Christian County, Ky., June 1, 1876
   d. February 5, 1928
   Governor of Tennessee, 1923-27

PETTIBONE, Augustus Herman
   Republican
   b. Bedford, Ohio, January 21, 1835
   d. Nashville, Tenn., November 26, 1918
   U. S. Representative, 1881-87

PEYTON, Balie
   Whig
   b. Gallatin, Tenn., November 26, 1803
   d. Gallatin, Tenn., August 18, 1878
   U. S. Representative, 1833-37

PEYTON, Joseph Hopkins
   Whig
   b. Gallatin, Tenn., May 20, 1808
   d. Gallatin, Tenn., November 11, 1845
   U. S. Representative, 1843-45

PHELAN, James
   Democrat
   b. Aberdeen, Miss., December 7, 1856
   d. Nassau, Bahama, January 30, 1891

U. S. Representative, 1887-91

PHILLIPS, Dayton Edward
    Republican
    b. Shell Creek, Tenn., March 29, 1910
    U. S. Representative, 1947-51

PIERCE, Rice Alexander
    Democrat
    b. Dresden, Tenn., July 3, 1848
    d. Union City, Tenn., July 12, 1936
    U. S. Representative, 1883-85, 1889-93,
        1897-1905

POLK, James Knox
    Democrat
    b. Little Sugar Creek, N. C., November 2, 1795
    d. Nashville, Tenn., June 15, 1849
    U. S. Representative, 1825-39; Speaker,
        1835-39
    Governor of Tennessee, 1839-41
    11th President of the United States, 1845-49

POLK, William Hawkins
    Democrat
    b. Maury County, Tenn., May 24, 1815
    d. Nashville, Tenn., December 16, 1862
    U. S. Representative, 1851-53

PORTER, James Davis, Jr.
    Democrat
    b. Paris, Tenn., December 7, 1828
    d. May 18, 1912
    Governor of Tennessee, 1875-79

POWELL, Samuel
    ----
    b. Norristown, Pa., July 10, 1776
    d. Rogersville, Tenn., August 2, 1841
    U. S. Representative, 1815-17

PRIEST, James Percy
    Democrat
    b. Carters Creek, Tenn., April 1, 1900
    d. Nashville, Tenn., October 12, 1956
    U. S. Representative, 1941-56

PROSSER, William Farrand
    Republican
    b. Williamsport, Pa., March 16, 1834
    d. Seattle, Wash., September 23, 1911
    U. S. Representative, 1869-71

QUARLES, James Minor
    Whig
    b. Louisa Court House, Va., February 8, 1823
    d. Nashville, Tenn., March 3, 1901
    U. S. Representative, 1859-61

QUILLEM, James H. (Jimmy)
    Republican
    b. Kingsport, Tenn., January 11, 1916
    U. S. Representative, 1963-

RANDOLPH, James Henry
    Republican
    b. Dandridge, Tenn., October 18, 1825
    d. Newport, Tenn., August 22, 1900
    U. S. Representative, 1877-79

READY, Charles
    Whig
    b. Readyville, Tenn., December 22, 1804
    d. Murfreesboro, Tenn., June 4, 1878
    U. S. Representative, 1853-59

REECE, Brazilla Carroll
    Republican
    b. Butler, Tenn., December 22, 1889
    d. Bethesda, Md., March 19, 1961
    U. S. Representative, 1921-31, 1933-47,
        1951-61
    Chairman Republican National Committee,
        1946-48

REECE, Louise Goff
    Republican
    b. Milwaukee, Wis., November 6, 1898
    d. Johnson City, Tenn., May 14, 1970
    U. S. Representative, 1961-63

REYNOLDS, James B.
    Democrat
    b. County Antrim, Ireland, 1779
    d. Montgomery County, Tenn., June 10, 1851
    U. S. Representative, 1815-17, 1823-25

RHEA, John
    Democrat
    b. Londonderry, Ireland, 1753
    d. Blountville, Tenn., May 27, 1832
    U. S. Representative, 1803-15, 1817-23

RICHARDSON, James Daniel
    Democrat
    b. Rutherford County, Tenn., March 10, 1843

d. Murfreesboro, Tenn., July 24, 1914
U. S. Representative, 1855-1905

RIDDLE, Haywood Yancey
    Democrat
    b. Van Buren, Tenn., June 20, 1834
    d. Lebanon, Tenn., March 28, 1829
    U. S. Representative, 1875-79

ROANE, Archibald
    Democrat-Republican
    b. Derry Township, Tenn., about 1759
    d. January 4, 1819
    Governor of Tennessee, 1801-03

ROBERTS, Albert H.
    Democrat
    b. Overton County, Tenn., July 4, 1868
    d. June 25, 1946
    Governor of Tennessee, 1919-21

RYE, Thomas Clark
    Democrat
    b. Camden, Tenn., June 2, 1863
    d. ----
    Governor of Tennessee, 1915-19

SALMON, William Charles
    Democrat
    b. Paris, Tenn., April 3, 1868
    d. Washington, D. C., May 13, 1925
    U. S. Representative, 1923-25

SANDERS, Newell
    Republican
    b. Bloomington, Ind., July 12, 1850
    d. Lookout Mountain, Tenn., January 26, 1939
    U. S. Senator, 1912-13

SANDFORD, James T.
    ----
    b. Virginia
    d. ----
    U. S. Representative, 1823-25

SAVAGE, John Houston
    ----
    b. McMinnville, Tenn., October 9, 1815
    d. McMinnville, Tenn., April 5, 1904
    U. S. Representative, 1849-53, 1855-59

SCOTT, Lon Allen
    Republican

b. Cypress Inn, Wayne County, Tenn.,
   September 25, 1888
d. Savannah, Tenn., February 11, 1931
U. S. Representative, 1921-23

SELLS, Sam Riley
Republican
b. Bristol, Tenn., August 2, 1871
d. Johnson City, Tenn., November 2, 1935
U. S. Representative, 1911-21

SENTER, DeWitt Clinton
Conservative Republican
Governor of Tennessee, 1867-71

SENTER, William Tandy
Whig
b. Bean Station, Tenn., May 12, 1801
d. Panther Springs, Tenn., August 28, 1848
U. S. Representative, 1843-45

SEVIER, John
Democrat (North Carolina/ Tennessee)
b. near Harrisonburg, Va., September 23, 1745
d. near Fort Decatur, Ala., September 24, 1815
U. S. Representative, 1789-91 (North Carolina)
Governor of Tennessee, 1796-1801, 1803-09
U. S. Representative, 1811-15 (Tennessee)

SHIELDS, Ebenezer J.
Whig
b. Georgia, December 22, 1778
d. near La Grange, April 21, 1846
U. S. Representative, 1835-39

SHIELDS, John Knight
Democrat
b. "Clinchdale" near Bean's Station, Tenn.,
   August 15, 1858
d. Clinchdale, near Knoxville, Tenn.,
   September 30, 1934
U. S. Senator, 1913-25

SIMONTON, Charles Bryson
Democrat
b. Tipton County, Tenn., September 8, 1838
d. Covington, Tenn., June 10, 1911
U. S. Representative, 1879-83

SIMS, Thetus Williette
Democrat

b. Waynesboro, Tenn., April 25, 1852
d. Washington, D. C., December 17, 1939
U. S. Representative, 1897-1921

SMITH, Daniel
b. Stafford County, Va., October 28, 1748
d. "Rock Castle" near Hendersonville, Tenn., June 6, 1818
U. S. Senator, 1798-99, 1805-09

SMITH, Samuel Axley
  Democrat
  b. Monroe County, Tenn., June 26, 1822
  d. Point Pleasant, Pa., November 25, 1863
  U. S. Representative, 1853-59

SMITH, William Jay
  Republican
  b. Birmingham, England, September 24, 1823
  d. Memphis, Tenn., November 29, 1913
  U. S. Representative, 1869-71

SNEED, William Henry
  American Party
  b. Davidson County, Tenn., August 27, 1812
  d. Knoxville, Tenn., September 18, 1869
  U. S. Representative, 1855-57

SNODGRASS, Charles Edward
  Democrat
  b. Sparta, Tenn., December 28, 1866
  d. Crossville, Tenn., August 3, 1936
  U. S. Representative, 1899-1903

SNODGRASS, Henry Clay
  Democrat
  b. Sparta, Tenn., March 29, 1848
  d. Altus, Okla., April 22, 1931
  U. S. Representative, 1891-95

STANDIFER, James
  Whig
  b. Sequatchie Valley near Dunlap, Tenn.
  d. Washington, D. C., August 20, 1837
  U. S. Representative, 1823-25, 1829-37

STANTON, Frederick Perry
  Democrat
  b. Alexandria, Va., December 22, 1814
  d. Stanton, Fla., June 4, 1894
  U. S. Representative, 1845-55
  Governor of Kansas Territory, 1859-61

STEWART, Arthur Thomas
    Democrat
    b. Dunlap. Tenn., January 11, 1892
    U.S. Senator, 1939-49

STOKES, William Brickly
    Republican
    b. Chatham County, N. C., September 9, 1814
    d. Alexandria, Tenn., March 14, 1897
    U. S. Representative, 1859-61 (Whig), 1866-71

STONE, William
    Whig
    b. Sevier County, Tenn. (then N. C.),
        January 26, 1791
    d. Delphi (later Davis), Tenn., February
        14, 1853
    U. S. Representative, 1837-39

SUTTON, James Patrick (Pat)
    Democrat
    b. Wartrace, Tenn., October 31, 1915
    U. S. Representative, 1949-55

TAYLOR, Alfred Alexander
    Republican
    b. Happy Valley, Tenn., August 6, 1848
    d. Johnson City, Tenn., November 25, 1931
    U. S. Representative, 1889-95
    Governor of Tennessee, 1921-23

TAYLOR, James Willis
    Republican
    b. Lead Mine Bend, Tenn., August 28, 1880
    d. LaFollette, Tenn., November 14, 1939
    U. S. Representative, 1919-39

TAYLOR, John May
    Democrat
    b. Lexington, Tenn., May 18, 1838
    d. Lexington, Tenn., February 17, 1911
    U. S. Representative, 1883-87

TAYLOR, Nathaniel Green
    Whig
    b. Happy Valley, Tenn., December 29, 1819
    d. Happy Valley, Tenn., April 1, 1887
    U. S. Representative, 1854-55, 1866-67

TAYLOR, Robert Love
    Democrat
    b. Happy Valley, Tenn., July 31, 1850
    d. Washington, D. C., March 31, 1912

U. S. Representative, 1879-81
Governor of Tennessee, 1887-91, 1897-99
U. S. Senator, 1907-12

TAYLOR, Zachary
    Republican
    b. Brownsville, Tenn., May 9, 1849
    d. Ellendale, Tenn., February 19, 1921
    U. S. Representative, 1885-87

THOMAS, Isaac
    Democrat
    b. Sevierville, Tenn., November 4, 1784
    d. Alexandria, La., February 2, 1859
    U. S. Representative, 1815-17

THOMAS, James Houston
    Democrat
    b. Iredell, N. C., September 22, 1808
    d. Fayetteville, Tenn., August 4, 1876
    U.S. Representative, 1847-51, 1859-61

THORNBURGH, Jacob Montgomery
    Republican
    b. New Market, Tenn., July 3, 1837
    d. Knoxville, Tenn., September 19, 1890
    U. S. Representative, 1873-79

TILLMAN, Lewis
    Republican
    b. Shelbyville, Tenn., August 18, 1816
    d. Shelbyville, Tenn., May 3, 1886
    U. S. Representative, 1869-71

TRIMBLE, John
    Republican
    b. Roane County, Tenn., February 7, 1812
    d. Nashville, Tenn., February 23, 1884
    U. S. Representative, 1867-69

TROUSDALE, William
    Democrat
    Governor of Tennessee, 1849-51

TURLEY, Thomas Battle
    Democrat
    b. Memphis, Tenn., April 5, 1845
    d. Memphis, Tenn., July 1, 1910
    U. S. Senator, 1897-1903

TURNER, Clarence Wyly
    Democrat
    b. Clydeton, Tenn., October 22, 1866

    d. Washington, D. C., March 23, 1939
    U. S. Representative, 1922-23, 1933-39

TURNEY, Hopkins Lacy
    Democrat
    b. Dixon Springs, Tenn., October 3, 1797
    d. Winchester, Tenn., August 1, 1857
    U. S. Representative, 1837-43
    U. S. Senator, 1845-51

TURNEY, Peter
    Democrat
    b. Jasper, Tenn., September 22, 1827
    d. 1903
    Governor of Tennessee, 1893-97

TYSON, Lawrence Davis
    Democrat
    b. Greenville, N. C., July 4, 1861
    d. Strafford, Pa., August 24, 1929
    U. S. Senator, 1925-29

VAUGHAN, William Wirt
    Democrat
    b. La Guardo (now Martha), Tenn., July 2, 1831
    d. Crockett Mills, near Alamo, Tenn., August 19, 1878
    U. S. Representative, 1871-73

WALTERS, Herbert S.
    Democrat
    b. Leadville, Tenn., November 17, 1891
    U. S. Senator, 1963-64

WARNER, Richard
    Democrat
    b. Chapel Hill, September 19, 1835
    d. Nashville, Tenn., March 4, 1915
    U. S. Representative, 1881-85

WASHINGTON, Joseph Edwin
    Democrat
    b. Cedar Hill, Tenn., November 10, 1851
    d. "Wessyngton," Robertson County, Tenn., August 28, 1915
    U. S. Representative, 1887-97

WATKINS, Albert Galiton
    Democrat
    b. Jefferson City, Tenn., May 5, 1818
    d. Mooresburg, Tenn., November 9, 1895
    U. S. Representative, 1849-53

WATTERSON, Harvey Magee
    Democrat
    b. "Beechgrove," Tenn., November 23, 1811
    d. Louisville, Ky., October 1, 1891
    U. S. Representative, 1839-43

WEAKLEY, Robert
    ----
    b. Halifax County, Va., July 20, 1764
    d. Nashville, Tenn., February 4, 1845
    U. S. Representative, 1809-11

WEBB, William Robert
    Democrat
    b. near Mount Tizrah, N. C., November 11, 1842
    d. Bell Buckle, Tenn., December 19, 1926
    U. S. Senator, 1913

WHARTON, Jesse
    ----
    b. Covesville, Va., July 29, 1782
    d. Nashville, Tenn., July 22, 1833
    U. S. Representative, 1807-09
    U. S. Senator, 1814-15

WHITE, Hugh Lawson
    ----
    b. Iredell County, N. C., October 30, 1773
    d. Knoxville, Tenn., April 10, 1840
    U. S. Senator, 1825-40; President pro
        tempore, 1832-33

WHITE, James
    ----
    b. Philadelphia, Pa., June 16, 1749
    d. Attakapas, La., October 1809
    Member Continental Congress (North Carolina),
        1786-88
    U. S. Representative (Territorial Delegate),
        1794-96

WHITESIDE, Jenkin
    ----
    b. Lancaster, Pa., 1772
    d. Lancaster, Pa., September 25, 1822
    U. S. Senator, 1809-11

WHITTHORNE, Washington Curran
    Democrat
    b. Farmington, Tenn., April 19, 1825
    d. Columbia, Tenn., September 21, 1891
    U. S. Representative, 1871-83
    U. S. Senator, 1886-87
    U. S. Representative, 1887-91

WILLIAMS, Christopher Harris
    Whig
    b. Hillsboro, N. C., December 18, 1798
    d. Lexington, Tenn., November 27, 1857
    U. S. Representative, 1837-43, 1849-53

WILLIAMS, John
    ----
    b. Surry County, N. C., January 29, 1778
    d. Knoxville, Tenn., August 10, 1837
    U. S. Senator, 1815-23

WILLIAMS, Joseph Lanier
    Whig
    b. Knoxville, Tenn., October 23, 1810
    d. Knoxville, Tenn., December 14, 1865
    U. S. Representative, 1837-43

WRIGHT, John Vines
    Democrat
    b. Purdy, Tenn., June 28, 1828
    d. Washington, D. C., June 11, 1908
    U. S. Representative, 1855-61

YOUNG, Hiram Casey
    Democrat
    b. Tuscaloosa, Ala., December 14, 1828
    d. Memphis, Tenn., August 17, 1899
    U. S. Representative, 1875-81, 1883-85

ZOLLICOFFER, Felix Kirk
    State Rights Whig
    b. Bigbyville, Tenn., May 19, 1812
    d. Mill Springs, Ky., January 19, 1862
    U. S. Representative, 1853-59

PROMINENT PERSONALITIES

The following select list of prominent persons of Tennessee has been selected to indicate the valuable contributions they have made to American life.

BARNARD, Edward Emerson
    b. Nashville, Tenn., December 16, 1857
    d. February 6, 1923
    Junior astronomer, Lick Observatory, 1887-95
    Astronomer, Yerkes Observatory, 1895-1923
    Discovered fifth satellite of Jupiter and the nebulous ring around Nova Aurigae

BRADFORD, Roark
    b. Lauderdale County, Tenn., August 21, 1896
    d. November 13, 1948
    Author: Ol' Man Adam An' His Chillun, 1928
        John Henry, 1931 (dramatized, 1940, with music by Jacques Wolfe)
        Let the Band Play Dixie, 1934
        The Three-Headed Angel, 1937

CLAXTON, Philander P.
    b. Bedford County, Tenn., September 28, 1862
    d. January 1957
    Professor of Education, University of Tennessee, 1902-11
    U. S. Commissioner of Education, 1911-21
    Chairman, National Student Forum on Paris Pact, 1929-38

DAVIS, Sam
    b. near Smyrna, Tenn., 1842
    d. by hanging, November 27, 1863
    Captured by Union forces and sentenced to hang

FARRAGUT, David Glasgow
    b. near Knoxville, Tenn., July 5, 1801
    d. August 14, 1870
    Served U. S. Navy
    Commanded West Gulf Blockading Squadron during Civil War
    Captured New Orleans, promoted to Rear Admiral, 1862
    Promoted to Admiral, 1866

FORREST, Nathan Bedford
    b. Bedford County, Tenn., July 13, 1821
    d. October 29, 1877
    Brigadier General, Confederate Army, 1862
    Major General, Confederate Army, 1863
    Lieutenant General, Confederate Army, 1865

HALLIBURTON, Richard
    b. Brownsville, Tenn., January 9, 1900
    d. 1900
    Climbed Matterhorn, 1921
    Swam Hellespont, 1925
    Swam Panama Canal, 1928
    Author: The Royal Road to Romance, 1925
            The Glorious Adventure, 1927
            New Worlds to Conquer, 1929
            Seven League Boots, 1935

HARRIS, George Washington ("Sut Lovinggood")
    b. Allegheny City, March 20, 1814
    d. Knoxville, Tenn., December 11, 1869
    Captain of steamer Knoxville
    Jeweler
    Contributor of Tennessee humor pieces to
        New York Spirit of the Times, 1843-57
    Author: The Sut Lovinggood Yarns, 1867

JONES, Jesse Holman
    b. Robertson County, Tenn., April 5, 1874
    d. June 1, 1956
    Organizer South Texas Lumber Company, 1902
    Organizer Texas Trust Company (now Bankers
        Mortgage Company), Houston, 1909

MOORE, Grace
    b. Jellicoe, Tenn., December 5, 1901
    d. in a plane crash, Copenhagen, Denmark,
        January 26, 1947
    Soprano
    Made debut in Metropolitan Opera Company in
        "La Boheme," February 7, 1928
    Revived French opera "Louise" by Charpentier,
        1939

ROBERTSON, James
    b. Brunswick County, Va., June 28, 1742
    d. Chickasaw Bluffs, Tenn., September
        1, 1814
    Fought in Lord Dunmore's War - Battle Point
        Pleasant, 1774
    Agent for North Carolina and Virginia to
        Cherokee Indians
    Brigadier General Territorial Government
        Southwest of Ohio to 1794
    Member Tennessee Constitutional Convention,
        1796
    Tennesseee Senator, 1798

SEQUOYA
    b. Loudon County, Tenn., 1770

d. probably at Tamaulipas, Mexico, August 1843
Completed table of 86 characters representing sounds of the Cherokee language, 1821
Taught many Indians to read and write their own language
Introduced system to Cherokees in Arkansas, 1822
Moved with Cherokees to Okla., 1828
Began publishing weekly paper in Cherokee, 1828
Envoy of Cherokees to Washington, D. C., 1828
Cherokee National Council granted him life-time pension, 1843
Sequoia redwood trees in California named for him

STRIBLING, Thomas Sigismund
    b. Clifton, Tenn., March 4, 1881
    d. Clifton, Tenn., July 8, 1965
    Author: *The Cruise of the Drydock*, 1917
        Birthright, 1922
        Fombombo, 1923
        Red Sand, 1924
        Bright Metal, 1928
        East Is East, 1928
        Strange Man, 1929

WALKER, William
    b. Nashville, Tenn., May 8, 1824
    d. by execution - firing squad, Trukillo, Honduras, September 12, 1860
    Went to California as part of gold rush
    Led American settlers in colonizing Mexican states of Sonora and Lower California - without permission of Mexico - landed at La Paz, proclaiming Lower California, independent republic, with himself as president, 1853

FIRST STATE CONSTITUTION

THE CONSTITUTION OF TENNESSEE—1796 *

We, the people of the territory of the United States south of the river Ohio, having the right of admission into the General Government as a member State thereof, consistent with the Constitution of the United States and the act of cession of the State of North Carolina, recognizing the ordinance for the government of the territory of the United States northwest of the river Ohio, do ordain and establish the following constitution or form of government, and do mutually agree with each other to form ourselves into a free and independent State by the name of the State of Tennessee.

ARTICLE I

SECTION 1. The legislative authority of this State shall be vested in a general assembly, which shall consist of a senate and house of representatives, both dependent on the people.

SEC. 2. Within three years after the first meeting of the general assembly, and within every subsequent term of seven years, an enumeration of the taxable inhabitants shall be made in such manner as shall be directed by law; the number of representatives shall, at the several periods of making such enumeration, be fixed by the legis-

---

* Journal of the Proceedings of a Convention begun and held at Knoxville, January 11, 1796. Knoxville: Printed by George Roulstone, 1796; Nashville: Reprinted by McKennie & Brown, True Whig Office, 1852. pp. 32.

lature, and apportioned among the several counties according to the number of taxable inhabitants in each, and shall never be less than twenty-two nor greater than twenty-six until the number of taxable inhabitants shall be forty thousand, and after that event at such ratio that the whole number of representatives shall never exceed forty.

Sec. 3. The number of senators shall, at the several periods of making the enumeration before mentioned, be fixed by the legislature and apportioned among the districts formed as hereinafter directed, according to the number of taxable inhabitants in each, and shall never be less than one-third nor more than one-half of the number of representatives.

Sec. 4. The senators shall be chosen by districts, to be formed by the legislature, each district containing such a number of taxable inhabitants as shall be entitled to elect not more than three senators. When a district shall be composed of two or more counties they shall be adjoining, and no county shall be divided in forming a district.

Sec. 5. The first election for senators and representatives shall commence on the second Thursday of March next, and shall continue for that and the succeeding day, and the next election shall commence on the first Thursday of August, one thousand seven hundred and ninety-seven, and shall continue on that and the succeeding day; and forever after elections shall be held once in two years, commencing on the first Thursday in August and terminating the succeeding day.

Sec. 6. The first session of the general assembly shall commence on the last Monday of March next; the second on the third Monday of September, one thousand seven hundred and ninety-seven; and forever after the general assembly shall meet on the third Monday of September next ensuing the then election, and at no other period, unless as provided for by this constitution.

Sec. 7. That no person shall be eligible to a seat in the general assembly unless he shall have resided three years in the State and one year in the county immediately preceding the election, and shall possess in his own right in the county which he represents not less than two hundred acres of land, and shall have attained to the age of twenty-one years.

Sec. 8. The senate and house of representatives, when assembled, shall each choose a speaker and its other officers, be judges of the qualifications and elections of its members, and sit upon its own adjournments from day to day. Two-thirds of each house shall constitute a quorum to do business, but a smaller number may adjourn from day to day, and may be authorized by law to compel the attendance of absent members.

Sec. 9. Each house may determine the rules of its proceedings, punish its members for disorderly behavior, and, with the concurrence of two-thirds expel a member, but not a second time for the same offence, and shall have all other powers necessary for the legislature of a free State.

Sec. 10. Senators and representatives shall, in all cases, except treason, felony, or breach of the peace, be privileged from arrest during the session of the general assembly, and in going to and returning from the same; and for any speech or debate in either house, they shall not be questioned in any other place.

Sec. 11. Each house may punish, by imprisonment, during their session, any person, not a member, who shall be guilty of disrespect to the house, by any disorderly or contemptuous behavior in their presence.

SEC. 12. When vacancies happen in either house, the governor, for the time being, shall issue writs of election to fill such vacancies.

SEC. 13. Neither house shall, during their session, adjourn without consent of the other, for more than three days, nor to any other place than that in which the two houses shall be sitting.

SEC. 14. Bills may originate in either house, but may be amended, altered, or rejected by the other.

SEC. 15. Every bill shall be read three times, on three different days, in each house, and be signed by the respective speakers, before it becomes a law.

SEC. 16. After a bill has been rejected, no bill containing the same substance shall be passed into a law during the same session.

SEC. 17. The style of the laws of this State shall be, *"Be it enacted by the general assembly of the State of Tennessee."*

SEC. 18. Each house shall keep a journal of its proceedings, and publish them, except such parts as the welfare of the State may require to be kept secret. And the yeas and nays of the members on any question shall, at the request of any two of them, be entered on the journals.

SEC. 19. The doors of each house, and committees of the whole, shall be kept open, unless when the business shall be such as ought to be kept secret.

SEC. 20. The legislature of this State shall not allow the following officers of government greater annual salaries than as follows, until the year one thousand eight hundred and four, to wit:

The governor not more than seven hundred and fifty dollars.

The judges of the superior courts not more than six hundred dollars each.

The secretary not more than four hundred dollars.

The treasurer or treasurers not more than 4 per cent. for receiving and paying out all moneys.

The attorney or attorneys for the State shall receive a compensation for their services, not exceeding fifty dollars for each superior court which he shall attend.

No member of the legislature shall receive more than one dollar and seventy-five cents per day, nor more for every twenty-five miles he shall travel in going to and returning from the general assembly.

SEC. 21. No money shall be drawn from the treasury but in consequence of appropriations made by law.

SEC. 22. No person who heretofore hath been, or hereafter may be, a collector or holder of public moneys shall have a seat in either house of the general assembly, until such person shall have accounted for, and paid into the treasury, all sums for which he may be accountable or liable.

SEC. 23. No judge of any court of law or equity, secretary of state, attorney-general, register, clerk of any court of record, or person holding any office under the authority of the United States shall have a seat in the general assembly; nor shall any person in this State hold more than one lucrative office at one and the same time: *Provided*, That no appointment in the militia, or to the office of a justice of the peace, shall be considered a lucrative office.

Sec. 24. No member of the general assembly shall be eligible to any office or place of trust, except to the office of a justice of the peace, or trustee of any literary institution, where the power of appointment to such office or place of trust is vested in their own body.

Sec. 25. Any member of either house of the general assembly shall have liberty to dissent from and protest against any act or resolve which he may think injurious to the public, or any individual, and have the reasons of his dissent entered on the journals.

Sec. 26. All lands liable to taxation in this State, held by deed, grant, or entry, shall be taxed equal and uniform, in such manner that no one hundred acres shall be taxed higher than another, except town-lots, which shall not be taxed higher than two hundred acres of land each; no freeman shall be taxed higher than one hundred acres, and no slave higher than two hundred acres on each poll.

Sec. 27. No article manufactured of the produce of this State shall be taxed otherwise than to pay inspection fees.

Article II

Section 1. The supreme executive power of this State shall be vested in a governor.

Sec. 2. The governor shall be chosen by the electors of the members of the general assembly, at the times and places where they shall respectively vote for the members thereof. The returns of every election for governor shall be sealed up, and transmitted to the seat of government by the returning officers, directed to the speaker of the senate, who shall open and publish them in the presence of a majority of the members of each house of the general assembly. The person having the highest number of votes shall be governor; but if two or more shall be equal and highest in votes, one of them shall be chosen governor by joint ballot of both houses of the general assembly. Contested elections for governor shall be determined by both houses of the general assembly, in such manner as shall be prescribed by law.

Sec. 3. He shall be at least twenty-five years of age, and possess a freehold estate of five hundred acres of land, and have been a citizen or inhabitant of this State four years next before his election, unless he shall have been absent on the public business of the United States or of this State.

Sec. 4. The first governor shall hold his office until the fourth Tuesday of September, one thousand seven hundred and ninety-seven, and until another governor shall be elected and qualified to office; and forever after the governor shall hold his office for the term of two years, and until another governor shall be elected and qualified; but shall not be eligible more than six years in any term of eight.

Sec. 5. He shall be commander-in-chief of the army and navy of this State, and of the militia, except when they shall be called into the service of the United States.

Sec. 6. He shall have power to grant reprieves and pardons, after conviction, except in cases of impeachment.

Sec. 7. He shall, at stated times, receive a compensation for his services, which shall not be increased or diminished during the period for which he shall have been elected.

Sec. 8. He may require information, in writing, from the officers in the executive department, upon any subject relating to the duties of their respective offices.

SEC. 9. He may, on extraordinary occasions, convene the general assembly by proclamation, and shall state to them, when assembled, the purpose for which they shall have been convened.

SEC. 10. He shall take care that the laws shall be faithfully executed.

SEC. 11. He shall, from time to time, give to the general assembly information of the state of the government, and recommend to their consideration such measures as he shall judge expedient.

SEC. 12. In case of his death, or resignation, or removal from office, the speaker of the senate shall exercise the office of governor until another governor shall be duly qualified.

SEC. 13. No member of Congress or person holding any office under the United States, or this State, shall execute the office of governor.

SEC. 14. When any officer, the right of whose appointment is by this constitution vested in the general assembly, shall, during the recess, die, or his office by other means become vacant, the governor shall have power to fill up such vacancy by granting a temporary commission, which shall expire at the end of the next session of the legislature.

SEC. 15. There shall be a seal of this State, which shall be kept by the governor, and used by him officially, and shall be called " The Great Seal of the State of Tennessee."

SEC. 16. All grants and commissions shall be in the name and by the authority of the State of Tennessee, be sealed with the State seal, and signed by the governor.

SEC. 17. A secretary of this State shall be appointed and commissioned during the term of four years. He shall keep a fair register of all the official acts and proceedings of the governor; and shall, when required, lay the same, and all papers, minutes, and vouchers relative thereto, before the general assembly, and shall perform such other duties as shall be enjoined him by law.

ARTICLE III

SECTION 1. Every freeman of the age of twenty-one years and upwards, possessing a freehold in the county wherein he may vote, and being an inhabitant of this State, and every freeman, being an inhabitant of any one county in the State six months immediately preceding the day of election, shall be entitled to vote for members of the general assembly, for the county in which he shall reside.

SEC. 2. Electors shall in all cases, except treason, felony, or breach of the peace, be privileged from arrest during their attendance at elections, and in going to and returning from them.

SEC. 3. All elections shall be by ballot.

ARTICLE IV

SECTION 1. The house of representatives shall have the sole power of impeachment.

SEC. 2. All impeachments shall be tried by the senate. When sitting for that purpose, the senators shall be upon oath or affirmation.

SEC. 3. No person shall be convicted, without the concurrence of two-thirds of the members of the whole house.

SEC. 4. The governor, and all civil officers under this State, shall be liable to impeachment for any misdemeanor in office; but judgment, in such cases, shall not extend further than to removal from office, and disqualification to hold any office of honor, trust, or profit under this State. The party shall, nevertheless, in all cases be liable to indictment, trial, judgment, and punishment, according to law.

Article V

SECTION 1. The judicial power of the State shall be vested in such superior and inferior courts of law and equity as the legislature shall, from time to time, direct and establish.

SEC. 2. The general assembly shall, by joint ballot of both houses, appoint judges of the several courts of law and equity, also an attorney or attorneys for the State, who shall hold their respective offices during good behavior.

SEC. 3. The judges of the superior court shall, at stated times, receive a compensation for their services, to be ascertained by law; but shall not be allowed any fees or perquisites of office, nor shall they hold any other office of trust or profit under this State or the United States.

SEC. 4. The judges of the superior courts shall be justices of oyer and terminer and general jail-delivery throughout the State.

SEC. 5. The judges of the superior and inferior courts shall not charge juries with respect to matters of fact, but may state the testimony and declare the law.

SEC. 6. The judges of the superior courts shall have power, in all civil cases, to issue writs of *certiorari*, to remove any cause, or a transcript thereof, from any inferior court of record into the superior, on sufficient cause, supported by oath or affirmation.

SEC. 7. The judges or justices of the inferior courts of law shall have power, in all civil cases, to issue writs of *certiorari*, to remove any cause, or a transcript thereof, from any inferior jurisdiction into their court, on sufficient cause, supported by oath or affirmation.

SEC. 8. No judge shall sit on the trial of any cause where the parties shall be connected with him by affinity or consanguinity, except by consent of parties. In case all the judges of the superior court shall be interested in the event of any cause, or related to all or either of the parties, the governor of the State shall in such case specially commission three men of law knowledge for the determination thereof.

SEC. 9. All writs and other process shall run in the name of the State of Tennessee, and bear test and be signed by the respective clerks. Indictments shall conclude, " against the peace and dignity of the State."

SEC. 10. Each court shall appoint its own clerk, who may hold his office during good behavior.

SEC. 11. No fine shall be laid on any citizen of this State that shall exceed fifty dollars, unless it shall be assessed by a jury of his peers, who shall assess the fine at the time they find the fact, if they think the fine ought to be more than fifty dollars.

SEC. 12. There shall be justices of the peace appointed for each county, not exceeding two for each captain's company, except for the company which includes the county town, which shall not exceed three, who shall hold their offices during good behavior.

Article VI

Section 1. There shall be appointed in each county, by the county court, one sheriff, one coroner, one trustee, and a sufficient number of constables, who shall hold their offices for two years. They shall also have power to appoint one register and ranger for the county, who shall hold their offices during good behavior. The sheriff and coroner shall be commissioned by the governor.

Sec. 2. There shall be a treasurer or treasurers appointed for the State, who shall hold his or their offices for two years.

Sec. 3. The appointment of all officers, not otherwise directed by this constitution, shall be vested in the legislature.

Article VII

Section 1. Captains, subalterns, and non-commissioned officers shall be elected by those citizens, in their respective districts, who are subject to military duty.

Sec. 2. All field-officers of the militia shall be elected by those citizens in their respective counties who are subject to military duty.

Sec. 3. Brigadiers-general shall be elected by the field-officers of their respective brigades.

Sec. 4. Majors-general shall be elected by the brigadiers and field-officers of the respective divisions.

Sec. 5. The governor shall appoint the adjutant-general; the majors-general shall appoint their aids; the brigadiers-general shall appoint their brigade-majors, and the commanding officers of regiments their adjutants and quartermasters.

Sec. 6. The captains and the subalterns of the cavalry shall be appointed by the troops enrolled in their respective companies, and the field-officers of the district shall be appointed by the said captains and subalterns: *Provided*, That, whenever any new county is laid off, that the field-officers of the said cavalry shall appoint the captain and other officers therein *pro tempore*, until the company is filled up and completed, at which time the election of the captains and subalterns shall take place as aforesaid.

Sec. 7. The legislature shall pass laws exempting citizens, belonging to any sect or denomination of religion the tenets of which are known to be opposed to the bearing of arms, from attending private and general musters.

Article VIII

Section 1. Whereas the ministers of the gospel are, by their professions, dedicated to God and the care of souls, and ought not to be diverted from the great duties of their functions; therefore no minister of the gospel, or priest of any denomination whatever, shall be eligible to a seat in either house of the legislature.

Sec. 2. No person who denies the being of God, or a future state of rewards and punishments, shall hold any office in the civil department of this State.

Article IX

Section 1. That every person who shall be chosen or appointed to any office of trust or profit shall, before entering on the execution thereof, take an oath to support the constitution of this State, and also an oath of office.

Sec. 2. That each member of the senate and house of representatives shall, before they proceed to business, take an oath or affirmation to support the constitution of this State, and also the following oath:

"I, A. B., do solemnly swear [or affirm] that, as a member of this general assembly, I will in all appointments vote without favor, affection, partiality, or prejudice, and that I will not propose or assent to any bill, vote, or resolution which shall appear to me injurious to the people, or consent to any act or thing whatever that shall have a tendency to lessen or abridge their rights and privileges, as declared by the constitution of this State."

Sec. 3. Any elector who shall receive any gift or reward for his vote, in meat, drink, money, or otherwise, shall suffer such punishment as the laws shall direct. And any person who shall directly or indirectly give, promise, or bestow any such reward to be elected, shall thereby be rendered incapable, for two years, to serve in the office for which he was elected, and be subject to such further punishment as the legislature shall direct.

Sec. 4. No new county shall be established by the general assembly which shall reduce the county or counties, or either of them, from which it shall be taken to a less content than six hundred and twenty-five square miles; nor shall any new county be laid off of less contents. All new counties, as to the right of suffrage and representation, shall be considered as a part of the county or counties from which it was taken, until entitled by numbers to the right of representation. No bill shall be passed into a law for the establishment of a new county except upon a petition to the general assembly for that purpose, signed by two hundred of the free male inhabitants within the limits or bounds of such new county prayed to be laid off.

Article X

Section 1. Knoxville shall be the seat of government until the year one thousand eight hundred and two.

Sec. 2. All laws and ordinances now in force and use in this Territory, not inconsistent with this constitution, shall continue to be in force and use in this State, until they shall expire, be altered, or repealed by the legislature.

Sec. 3. That whenever two-thirds of the general assembly shall think it necessary to amend or change this constitution, they shall recommend to the electors, at the next election for members to the general assembly, to vote for or against a convention; and if it shall appear that a majority of all the citizens of the State, voting for representatives, have voted for a convention, the general assembly shall, at their next session, call a convention, to consist of as many members as there be in the general assembly, to be chosen in the same manner, at the same place, and by the same electors that chose the general assembly, who shall meet within three months after the said election, for the purpose of revising, amending, or changing the constitution.

Sec. 4. The declaration of rights hereto annexed is declared to be a part of the constitution of this State, and shall never be violated on any pretence whatever. And to guard against transgressions of the high powers which we have delegated, we declare that everything in the bill of rights contained, and every other right not hereby delegated, is excepted out of the general powers of government, and shall forever remain inviolate.

Article XI

DECLARATION OF RIGHTS

Section 1. That all power is inherent in the people, and all free governments are founded on their authority, and instituted for their peace, safety, and happiness; for the advancement of those ends, they have at all times an unalienable and indefeasible right to alter, reform, or abolish the government in such manner as they may think proper.

Sec. 2. That, government being instituted for the common benefit, the doctrine of non-resistance against arbitrary power and oppression is absurd, slavish, and destructive to the good and happiness of mankind.

Sec. 3. That all men have a natural and indefeasible right to worship Almighty God according to the dictates of their own consciences; that no man can of right be compelled to attend, erect, or support any place of worship, or to maintain any ministry against his consent; that no human authority can in any case whatever control or interfere with the rights of conscience; and that no preference shall ever be given by law to any religious establishments or modes of worship.

Sec. 4. That no religious test shall ever be required as a qualification to any office or public trust under this State.

Sec. 5. That elections shall be free and equal.

Sec. 6. That the right of trial by jury shall remain inviolate.

Sec. 7. That the people shall be secure in their persons, houses, papers, and possessions, from unreasonable searches and seizures, and that general warrants, whereby an officer may be commanded to search suspected places, without evidence of the fact committed, or to seize any person or persons not named, whose offences are not particularly described and supported by evidence, are dangerous to liberty, and ought not to be granted.

Sec. 8. That no freeman shall be taken, or imprisoned, or disseized of his freehold, liberties, or privileges, or outlawed or exiled, or in any manner destroyed or deprived of his life, liberty, or property, but by the judgment of his peers or the law of the land.

Sec. 9. That in all criminal prosecutions the accused hath a right to be heard by himself and his counsel; to demand the nature and cause of the accusation against him, and to have a copy thereof; to meet the witnesses face to face; to have compulsory process for obtaining witnesses in his favor; and in prosecutions by indictment or presentment a speedy public trial, by an impartial jury of the county or district in which the crime shall have been committed; and shall not be compelled to give evidence against himself.

Sec. 10. That no person shall, for the same offence, be twice put in jeopardy of life or limb.

Sec. 11. That laws made for the punishment of facts committed previous to the existence of such laws, and by them only declared criminal, are contrary to the principles of a free government; wherefore no *ex post facto* law shall be made.

SEC. 12. That no conviction shall work corruption of blood or forfeiture of estate. The estate of such persons as shall destroy their own lives shall descend or vest as in case of natural death. If any person be killed by casualty, there shall be no forfeiture in consequence thereof.

SEC. 13. That no person arrested, or confined in jail, shall be treated with unnecessary rigor.

SEC. 14. That no freeman shall be put to answer any criminal charge, but by presentment, indictment, or impeachment.

SEC. 15. That all prisoners shall be bailable by sufficient sureties, unless for capital offences, when the proof is evident or the presumption great. And the privilege of the writ of *habeas corpus* shall not be suspended, unless when, in case of rebellion or invasion, the public safety may require it.

SEC. 16. That excessive bail shall not be required, nor excessive fines imposed, nor cruel and unusual punishments inflicted.

SEC. 17. That all courts shall be open; and every man, for an injury done him in his lands, goods, person, or reputation, shall have remedy by due course of law, and right and justice administered without sale, denial, or delay. Suits may be brought against the State in such manner and in such courts as the legislature may by law direct: *Provided*, The right of bringing suit be limited to the citizens of this State.

SEC. 18. That the person of a debtor, where there is not strong presumption of fraud, shall not be continued in prison after delivering up his estate for the benefit of his creditor or creditors, in such manner as shall be prescribed by law.

SEC. 19. That the printing-presses shall be free to every person who undertakes to examine the proceedings of the legislature, or of any branch or officer of government; and no law shall ever be made to restrain the right thereof. The free communication of thoughts and opinions is one of the invaluable rights of man; and every citizen may freely speak, write, and print on any subject, being responsible for the abuse of that liberty. But in prosecutions for the publication of papers investigating the official conduct of officers or men in public capacity, the truth thereof may be given in evidence; and in all indictments for libels, the jury shall have a right to determine the law and the facts, under the direction of the court, as in other cases.

SEC. 20. That no retrospective law, or law impairing the obligation of contracts, shall be made.

SEC. 21. That no man's particular services shall be demanded or property taken, or applied to public use, without the consent of his representatives, or without just compensation being made therefor.

SEC. 22. That the citizens have a right, in a peaceable manner, to assemble together for their common good, to instruct their representatives, and to apply to those invested with the powers of government for redress of grievances, or other proper purposes, by address or remonstrance.

SEC. 23. That perpetuities and monopolies are contrary to the genius of a free State, and shall not be allowed.

SEC. 24. That the sure and certain defence of a free people is a well-regulated militia; and as standing armies, in time of peace, are dangerous to freedom, they ought to be avoided, as far as the circumstances and safety of the community will admit, and that in all cases the military shall be in strict subordination to the civil authority.

SEC. 25. That no citizen in this State, except such as are employed in the Army of the United States or militia in actual service, shall be subject to corporal punishment under the martial law.

SEC. 26. That the freemen of this State have a right to keep and to bear arms for their common defence.

SEC. 27. That no soldier shall in time of peace be quartered in any house without consent of the owner, nor in time of war but in a manner prescribed by law.

SEC. 28. That no citizen of this State shall be compelled to bear arms, provided he will pay an equivalent, to be ascertained by law.

SEC. 29. That an equal participation of the free navigation of the Mississippi is one of the inherent rights of the citizens of this State; it cannot, therefore, be conceded to any prince, potentate, power, person, or persons whatever.

SEC. 30 That no hereditary emoluments, privileges, or honors shall ever be granted or conferred in this State.

SEC. 31. That the people residing south of French Broad and Holston, between the rivers Tennessee and the Big Pigeon, are entitled to the right of preëmption and occupancy in that tract.

SEC. 32. That the limits and boundaries of this State be ascertained, it is declared they are as hereafter mentioned; that is to say: Beginning on the extreme height of the Stone Mountain, at the place where the line of Virginia intersects it, in latitude thirty-six degrees and thirty minutes north; running thence along the extreme height of the said mountain to the place where Watauga River breaks through it; thence a direct course to the top of the Yellow Mountain, where Bright's road crosses the same; thence along the ridge of said mountain, between the waters of Doe River and the waters of Rock Creek, to the place where the road crosses the Iron Mountain; from thence along the extreme height of said mountain to where Nolichucky River runs through the same; thence to the top of the Bald Mountain; thence along the extreme height of said mountain to the Painted Rock, on French Broad River; thence along the highest ridge of said mountain to the place where it is called the Great Iron or Smoky Mountain; thence along the extreme height of said mountain to the place where it is called Unicoi or Unaka Mountain, between the Indian towns of Cowee and Old Chota; thence along the main ridge of the said mountain to the southern boundary of this State, as described in the act of cession of North Carolina to the United States of America, and that all the territory, lands, and waters lying west of the said line, as before mentioned, and contained within the chartered limits of the State of North Carolina, are within the boundaries and limits of this State, over which the people have the right of exercising sovereignty and right of soil so far as is consistent with the Constitution of the United States, recognizing the Articles of Confederation, the Bill of Rights, and constitution of North Carolina, the cession act of the said State, and the ordinance of the late Congress for the government of the territory northwest of the Ohio; provided nothing herein contained shall extend to affect the claim or claims of individuals to any part of the soil which is recognized to them by the aforesaid cession act.

Schedule

Section 1. That no inconvenience may arise from a change of the temporary to a permanent State government, it is declared that all rights, actions, prosecutions, claims, and contracts, as well of individuals as of bodies-corporate, shall continue as if no change had taken place in the administration of government.

Sec. 2. All fines, penalties, and forfeitures, due and owing to the territory of the United States of America south of the river Ohio, shall inure to the use of the State. All bonds for performance, executed to the governor of the said territory, shall be and pass over to the governor of this State, and his successors in office, for the use of the State, or by him or them respectively to be assigned over to the use of those concerned, as the case may be.

Sec. 3. The governor, secretary, judges, and brigadiers-general have a right, by virtue of their appointments, under the authority of the United States, to continue in the exercise of the duties of their respective offices in their several departments until the said officers are superseded under the authority of this constitution.

Sec. 4. All officers, civil and military, who have been appointed by the governor, shall continue to exercise their respective offices until the second Monday in June, and until successors in office shall be appointed under the authority of this constitution and duly qualified.

Sec. 5. The governor shall make use of his private seal until a State seal shall be provided.

Sec. 6. Until the first enumeration shall be made, as directed in the second section of the first article of this constitution, the several counties shall be respectively entitled to elect one senator and two representatives: *Provided*, That no new county shall be entitled to separate representation previous to taking the enumeration.

Sec. 7. That the next election for representatives and other officers to be held for the county of Tennessee shall be held at the house of William Miles.

Sec. 8. Until a land-office shall be opened, so as to enable the citizens south of French Broad and Holston, between the rivers Tennessee and Big Pigeon, to obtain titles upon their claims of occupancy and preëmption, those who hold land by virtue of such claims shall be eligible to serve in all capacities where a freehold is by this constitution made a requisite qualification.

Done in convention at Knoxville, by unanimous consent, on the sixth day of February, in the year of our Lord one thousand seven hundred and ninety-six, and of the Independence of the United States of America the twentieth. In testimony whereof we have hereunto subscribed our names.

William Blount, *President.*

William Maclin, *Secretary.*

SELECTED DOCUMENTS

The documents selected for this section have been chosen to reflect the interests or attitudes of the contemporary observer or writer. Documents relating specifically to the constitutional development of Tennessee will be found in volume nine of <u>Sources and Documents of United States Constitutions</u>, a companion reference collection to the Columbia University volumes previously cited.

TENNESSEE DURING THE CIVIL WAR

Edward Dicey presents an interesting description of the state in the midst of the Civil War.

Source: Edward Dicey. **Six Months in the Federal States**. London and Cambridge: Macmillan and Co., 1863.

THE road from Louisville to Nashville lay right on the track of the war, through Kentucky and Western Tennessee. The railroad had only been re-opened ten days or so before I passed over it. The Confederate forces had been till quite recently in possession of Nashville, and the first great battle of the Western campaign had been expected to take place along the railroad, at Bowling Green station, and would doubtless have taken place there, had not the Confederates evacuated the position on the advance of the Union troops. Still, the traces of the recent war, and of the march and retreat of great armies, were not so numerous as I expected. Where houses are so few and far between as they are in these new States, and where so much of the country is still uncultivated, it is difficult, even for wanton destruction, to produce much outward appearance of desolation; and, besides, from the nature of this civil war, both armies in these border States have proceeded on the assumption, that they were in a friendly country, and have, therefore, as a rule, spared private property. Yet there were evidences enough of the war, after all. Along a line of some hundred and eighty odd miles, there was not a bridge that had not been burnt or broken down. Rickety wooden structures, which made a stranger tremble at the idea of passing over them, had been run up in their stead, and small detachments of Union soldiers were posted by these make-shift bridges to preserve them from destruction. The rails had often been torn up, for many hundred yards together, and the cars run over a newly-laid down trackway, side by side with the old line of rails. There were broken engines, too, and burnt cars lying alongside the line; and, wherever there were the traces of a Confederate encampment, there the blackened ruins of the roadside houses told you of the reckless destruction worked by the retreating army in the despair of defeat. The great Confederate fort of Bowling Green struck me, on a rapid view, as of no great military strength. But, long after the war is over, the earthworks of the camp on the Green River, and the shattered buttresses of the grand stone arches, will remain as tokens of the great insurrection.

But, in truth, this Tennessee country is so bright and pleasant a one, that it would take years of war to make it look other than prosperous, especially above all other seasons, in the early and short-lived bloom of a Southern spring. My impression of Tennessee, like most of one's impressions about the localities of the Southern States, was taken from the old nigger melody of the darkie who fell in love with the "lovely Rosa Lee, courting down in Tennessee." For once the impression was a correct one; and, of all pleasant places to go courting in, it would be "down in Tennessee," in that sweet April time. As far as country goes, I should be hard put to choose, if I had to fix my dwelling-place in Ohio or in Tennessee. In the latter State the climate is softer, and more Southern; but there is less life, less energy, perhaps, about the Slave State—less sign of rapid progress. The fields are worked by gangs of negroes. Every now and then, too, you see the wretched wood hovels, telling of actual poverty—things which you do not see in Ohio; and, also, I grieve to say, when you look closely into the Tennessee paradise, the garden of Eden is somewhat of a dirty one.

Of all American cities, which I have seen, Nashville, or "Naseville," as they call it, in the soft Southern lisp, is the most picturesque. Perched upon a high steep ridge hanging over the Cumberland river, the "Rocky City" is perforce divorced from that dismal rectangular system so fatal to the beauty of American towns. The streets run up and down all sorts of slopes, and at all kinds of angles. The rows of houses stand terrace-like one above the other; and, highest of all, the State Capitol towers grandly above the city. The main thoroughfares are broad and bright, shaded over pleasantly by the rows of lime and chestnut trees, which grow on either side. All round the city, on every inequality of the broken ground, there are placed well-built stone villas, and the whole place had a sort of New World Bath air about it, which struck me curiously.

In happier days, Nashville must have been a very pleasant dwelling-place; but when I saw it, the whole aspect of the city was, even for a stranger, a dreary and dismal one. An American—a staunch Union man himself—described its state as being like that of Italian cities he had seen, shortly after the Austrians re-occupied them in '49. But, I own, to me this description seemed, externally, rather overdrawn. I should say myself that Nashville looked more like a city still stunned by the blow of some great public calamity. Outwardly, it had not suffered much from its various military occupations. The Louisville trains stopped on the northern side of the river, at Edgefield, for the great railway-bridge which spanned the Cumberland was blown up by the Confederates on leaving. With a reckless wantonness, the beautiful suspension bridge was cut to pieces at the same period, so that all communication between Nashville and the North had to be carried on by boats and ferries. Otherwise, the city had received little material injury; but I think this absence of external ruin rather increased the effect of the general depression visible throughout the town. When Mr. Seward went over to Winchester, on its first occupation by General Banks' division, Mr. Sumner, who had often disputed with him as to the existence of a strong Union sentiment in the South, asked him what he thought of the look of things at the Virginian town?

" Well," he answered, "all the men were gone to the "war, and all the women were she-devils." The same description would not, I suspect, have applied badly to Nashville. The town had a deserted air. If you took away the Union soldiers, there would have been very few people about the streets at all. There were numbers of negroes, apparently idling about the town, but the white population seemed scanty for the size of the place. Young men you met very seldom about—and, indeed, the proportion of women to men was unusually large. What is stranger still, the children seemed to have been sent away. At any rate, contrary to the custom of other American towns, they were not visible in the streets. The Union regiments quartered here were from the neighbouring States, and, one would suppose, would have had many acquaintances in the town, but there was, avowedly, little intercourse between the military and the inhabitants, while the soldiers complained bitterly of the manner in which the Nashville women expressed their dislike on every possible occasion. Half the shops were closed, and in the few of any size still open the owners sat moodily among empty shelves. Trade, however, was gradually reviving. In every shop there were notices put up of "no Southern money taken:" and the shopkeepers seemed willing enough to sell what goods they had at exorbitant prices to the Federal soldiers. On the walls there still hung the tattered half-torn-down official notices of the Confederate government, and on a building right in front of the hotel where I lodged you could still read an inscription over the door, "Head Quarters of the Confederate States' Army," while displayed openly in the windows of the stationers, I saw copies of patriotic Confederate dance music, headed "the Confederate Prize Banner Quadrille," "the Lady Polk Polka," and the "Morgan Schottische." Of any pro-Union exhibition of feeling on the part of private individuals I could see little trace. Over the public buildings the stars and stripes floated gaily; but on no single dwelling-house could I see an

Union flag. In the shop windows there were no prints of Federal victories, no display of the patriotic books and pamphlets so universal throughout the North. In the way of business, indeed, nothing seemed stirring, unless it was the undertaking trade, which, from the number of coffins I saw about, ought to have been thriving. Of the women I met, a majority were in deep mourning, not so much, I fear, as an exhibition of political sentiment, as in memory of husbands, and sons, and brothers, who had fallen on the slaughter field of Pittsburgh Landing. Martial law was not enforced, but after dark the streets were almost deserted; sentries were posted at frequent intervals, and ever and anon the death-like stillness of the town was broken by the jangle of swords and spurs, as the mounted patrols rode slowly past. The theatre had been re-opened, more, I should fancy, from political motives than from any prospect of pecuniary profit. The house was almost exclusively filled with Federal soldiers, and on the two occasions when I went there I only saw one lady amongst the audience, and she was a Frenchwoman. The wealthier inhabitants were daily leaving the town, on account of the general depression which prevailed there. Politics seemed to be a tabooed subject in private conversation. In several houses that I went into, I found that the heads of the family were under arrest, and there were constant rumours, though I believe mostly exaggerated ones, of collisions between the inhabitants and the soldiery. All bar-rooms were closed by military orders, a circumstance which must in itself have been a bitter grievance to a liquor-loving, bar-frequenting people, and neither for love nor money could a stranger obtain a drink more intoxicating than lager beer within the bounds of Nashville.

The press of Nashville represented, curiously enough, the disorganized condition of society. The editors of the old local papers, who were all bitter Secessionists, had left the town at the approach of the Federal forces, and their papers were either suspended or suppressed. The existing press of Nashville consisted of two small single sheet papers, the *Nashville Union* and the *Nashville Dispatch*. The former, of course, was the official organ of the Government. Commercially, I should question its having been a paying property, as every day there appeared piteous appeals to the loyal men of Tennessee to support " the uncompromising organ of Union," by sending in subscriptions and advertisements, and thus " to keep the flag of the Union, of law and order, streaming defiantly in the very face of the enemy, as he retires sullenly to the Gulf." One great object of the paper professed to be " to bring to light hundreds of crimes and outrages " committed by the rebels during their ascendancy, and " which the guilty authors believed would never be " brought to light." This part of its programme was amply redeemed, for the greater part of its meagre reading matter consisted of revelations of Confederate misrule, during the last few months. The stories quoted and the comments on them reminded me constantly of the revelations of Austrian and Papal cruelties, which used to be published in the Italian papers after the revolution of 1859, except that, to do the Confederates justice, in none of the documents quoted was there much proof of great personal cruelties. It is, I admit, extremely illegal and tyrannical to exile and imprison men on mere suspicion, to force recruits against their will into the ranks, and to confiscate property devoted to charitable purposes. But necessity knows no law, and if it was justifiable for the State of Tennessee to secede at all, I hardly think the steps by which the insurrectionary government sought to carry out the revolution, were in themselves crimes of any very deep dye. This, however, naturally enough, was not the opinion of the *Union*. The Confederate Government of Nashville appropriated two million dollars, belonging to the public school fund, for the purposes of the war, and on this outrage the *Union* harped perpetually in a series of short paragraphs, of which the following are average specimens:—

"Why should a child treat a rebel teacher with "respect? That teacher is the servile follower of "rebel leaders, who, to the disgrace of humanity, "plundered the noble fund of two million dollars, "which this State had created as an inviolable legacy "for the education of her children. Shame on such "villany!"

"The rebel government and rebel legislature of "Tennessee plunged their hands into the charity fund "of the State's poor children, and took from it two "million of dollars to purchase for themselves an "eternal infamy."

"Every time a rebel teacher sets foot in a school-"room, the robbed and plundered children should "rise from their seats and cry, 'Give us back the two "million dollars, which the State provided for our "education, and which your political idols stole from "us. Give it back! Give it back!'"

And so on indefinitely. The regular leaders were alternate attacks on the Secession movement and on the Abolitionists, though, as the paper is a Government organ, and subsidized by the Government, no attacks were allowed on the President or on his Administration. To the credit, too, of the *Union*, I should state that even in a period of such excitement, and in a paper conducted with such vehemence, there were no personal assaults on private individuals, no denunciations by name of suspected Secessionists. The advertisements were very few in number, and what there were were chiefly official ones. In fact the majority were notices of runaway slaves detained in the county gaol. It seemed strange to an Englishman to read a long string of advertisements like the following:—

"On the 8th day of May, 1862, I will expose to "public sale to the highest bidder, for cash, at the "Court House, Yard Gate, in Nashville, one negro "boy named William, levied on as the property of "Sharp and Hamilton, to satisfy sundry executions in

" my hands."

Again, amongst the committals to the gaol I came across the following :—

"April 21, 1862. A negro woman, who says her name is Lucinda, and belongs to William Donaldson, of Davidson County. The said woman is about 28 or 30 years old; dark copper colour."

"April 18, 1862. A negro man, who says his name is Andrew. Says he belongs to R. L. Brown, of Davidson county. Dark copper colour. Scar on the left side of his cheek. About 28 years old. Weighs about 158 pounds, and is 5 ft. 7 in. high." And at the end of each advertisement the owner is requested "to come forward, prove property, and pay charges, as the law directs." Then there were the advertisements of free negroes, confined to gaol on the suspicion of being runaways. Thus :—

"March 16, 1862. A negro man, says his name is George Mosely. Says he is a free man of colour. Says he lives in Indianopolis, in Indiana. About 37 years old. Weighs about 187 pounds. Has whiskers and a moustache, a small scar on corner of left eye. Dark copper colour, 5 ft. 10 in. high."

In fact, if it were not for the "peculiar institution," the advertisement department of the *Union* would be but shabbily provided.

The principles of the *Nashville Dispatch* were, according to the statement of its rival, "as nearly secessionist as it can be to keep out of Johnson's clutches," and the accusation was probably well founded. It was obviously written to suit a public to whom the successes of the Union were, to say the least, uninteresting. It professed no political principles, but it contained no prognostication of Federal victories, and, in fact, seemed disposed to ignore secession generally. I always believed that the *Giornale di Roma* had an unrivalled talent for conveying the minimum of news in a given number of columns, but I think the *Nashville*

Dispatch was no unworthy rival in the same laudable endeavour. What little news it gave, was composed of items of southern intelligence, reprinted from the northern papers, and, except in the official telegrams, the name "rebel" was never used, but always supplied by that of "Confederate." The leaders were generally on miscellaneous subjects, utterly disconnected with the war, and often consisted of short moral discourses on the benefits of forbearance and strict integrity. The trade advertisements were rather more numerous than those of the *Union*, but it had not the official ones of negro sales or committals to gaol. The space lost in this way was filled with a romantic story of love and seduction. Of the two, there was more "grit," to use a Yankee phrase, about the *Union*.

The whole policy, or rather want of policy, of the Federal government, with regard to the reconquered States, was exhibited at Nashville in its practical working. To suppress the rebellion was the one idea that either government or people had been able to grasp as yet; and, with regard to the future, the only vestige of a policy adopted was a general intention to restore, as much as might be, the *status quo* before the war. As soon as Nashville was retaken, Mr. Andrew Johnson was sent there as military governor. A Tennessee man himself, and a slaveholder, he was selected for the post, not only on account of his unswerving adherence to the Union, but because it was considered that his appointment would be a guarantee to the people of Tennessee that no violent interference with their property was designed. For the immediate purpose of pacification, the appointment was a wise one. Every step, consistent with a vigorous suppression of active secession, was taken to win back the allegiance of the people, and, as far as the language of the governor went, nothing could be more satisfactory to a slave-owning State. At the period of my visit, when reviewing a Minnesota regiment, quartered at Nashville (Minnesota, be it remembered, is a free State), Governor

Johnson used these words:—

"It had been charged by the apostles of treason that the North had come here to set negroes free. He knew the North, had travelled among her people, and he repelled the charge with scorn. There were abolition fanatics there, it was true—sectionalists, traitors, brothers of Southern secessionists—but these creatures constituted but a fraction of the great body of the North. The voice of the overwhelming mass of the North, as well as of nine men out of ten who stood before him was, 'We care nothing for your negroes. Manage them as best suits yourselves, but the Union shall be preserved, and you must obey the laws;'" and, according to the official report, this enunciation of principles was loudly cheered by the soldiers.

How far this patchwork policy will prove ultimately successful in re-establishing a pro-Union feeling, time alone can show. It had had little time to act, when I was at Nashville, and it was hard to judge what progress it had made. There was, indeed, no disguising the fact that the Federal Government had not received the sympathy it counted upon in Tennessee. The belief in the North had been that the Union armies would have been hailed as deliverers by a large portion of the population, but, hitherto, they had met, at the best, with a sullen acquiescence. It should be added, that the Union party made no attempt to represent things as more favourable than they were, and confessed the absence of Union sympathy as frankly as they admitted all their other failures and shortcomings. Indeed, the best sign, nationally, I saw about the Americans was the resolute fearlessness with which they looked facts in the face, even when telling against themselves. Thus, in Nashville, the Government party admitted openly, that since the occupation there had been no public expression of any love for the Union exhibited in this part of Tennessee. As evidences of returning loyalty, the *Nashville Union* quoted, I remember, with great pride, how one old lady had sent a

Federal flag to the Governor, with the request that it might be hung up in some public spot; and how the city council had at last, after nearly a month's deliberation, passed a resolution, that "they cordially thanked "the officers and soldiers of the United States for the "unexampled kindness and courtesy hitherto extended "to their fellow-citizens, and that as men striving in "the common work of re-establishing the Government "of their fathers, they pledged their most sincere and "hearty co-operation."

It was impossible to help feeling, that if the Unionists were gratified by demonstrations of such doubtful loyalty, they were easily contented. Of any practical manifestation of Union feeling there was little indication. With East Tennessee and Memphis still in the possession of the enemy, there could be no question as yet about how the Senators and Representatives of Tennessee were to be elected, and therefore, for the moment, this difficult question was postponed; but extreme difficulty had been already experienced in filling up the civil offices with loyal men. The corporation, by rather an arbitrary stretch of power, was required to take the oath of allegiance to the United States; and the greatest reluctance was exhibited by them in acceding to the requisition. For three weeks after Governor Johnson arrived, it was found impossible to induce any one to undertake the office of postmaster; and a yet longer period elapsed before an editor could be found bold enough to conduct a Government newspaper.

However, this absence of Union feeling was not so strange nor so disheartening as it might appear at first sight. There can be no doubt that the common people of Tennessee, like the inhabitants of all the Southern States, believed sincerely that the "Lincoln hordes" were coming down to destroy their property, burn their houses, and murder their wives and children. Extraordinary as such an illusion was, it could be accounted for partly by the comparative isolation of the South, partly by the extent to which the lower classes received all their intelligence and all their opinions from their leaders, and, still more, by the morbid nervousness which the existence of a slave population is sure to beget amongst the dominant race. By degrees the people of Tennessee were becoming convinced that the Northerners had no intention of interfering with their property, or of treating them as subjects of a conquered country; and that, in fact, life and property were far safer under a Federal Government than they had been under the Confederate rule. Again, the war was too near at hand, and the danger too imminent for Tennessee to appreciate fully that the battle had been fought and lost. It was easy enough for an indifferent spectator in the North to see that the Confederates were fighting a losing fight in the border States, and that even a return of fortune to their arms would only prolong a hopeless struggle; but, to men living in Tennessee, it was not so easy to take a wide view of the case. If Beauregard had won the battle of Pittsburgh Landing, or had defeated the Federals at Corinth, it was quite possible, though not probable, that Nashville might have been re-occupied for the time by the Confederates; and their return would have been the sure signal for a reign of terror of which all, who had given in their adhesion to the new Government, might reasonably have feared to be the victims. Moreover—and I believe this to have been the chief explanation—as long as the war lasts there can be no cordial restoration of Union feeling in any Southern State. Men may grow convinced of the folly of secession, may even wish for the triumph of the Union; but their hearts must be, after all, with the side for which their kinsmen and friends are fighting. I suppose there is hardly a family in Tennessee which has not some member in the ranks of the Confederate army. It is this conflict of affections which makes all civil war so hateful. How hateful it is, in truth, never came home to me till I saw it actually. I have known myself of a wife whose husband was fighting for the South, while her father and brother were in the Federal army. I knew, too, of a mother who had only two sons, one in the North, and the other in the South, both fighting in the armies that were ranged opposite to each other in front of Yorktown. So I, or any one, could name a hundred instances of father fighting against son—brother against brother—of families divided—of homes where there was mourning whenever the news of battle came, no matter which side had won the victory. I have dwelt thus somewhat at length on the reasons why I think the sullen attitude of Tennessee might be accounted for, because I am anxious not to convey the impression that I believe in the Southern or rather the Confederate doctrine of an innate and unconquerable aversion between the North and South. If once the insurrection were suppressed, and order restored, I have little doubt the Southern States would acquiesce in what was inevitable. There is no difference in race, or language, or religion, or geographical position to keep the two divisions of the Union apart. Whether the difference in domestic institutions would prove an insuperable cause of disunion, I cannot say. If it should so prove, the North will suppress or remove this cause, before it consents to the disruption of the Union. This is the only fact of which I feel positive.

In old English books about travel in Switzerland, it used to be a stock remark that you could tell whether a canton was Protestant or Catholic by the relative cleanliness or dirtiness of the towns. How far the fact was true, or how far, if true, it established the truth of the Protestant religion, I could never determine; but a similar conclusion may certainly be drawn with regard to the Free and the Slave States. You may lay it down as a rule throughout America, that wherever you find slavery, there you have dirt also. Nashville, as I said before, is one of the cleanest and brightest of towns at a distance; but when you come close the illusion vanishes. There is no excuse there for want of cleanliness. The position of the town makes drainage easy; the stone used so plentifully is clean of itself; and water is abundant. The only thing wanting seemed to be energy to keep the place clean. The hotel where I was stopping was in itself an institution (in American phrase) of the country. It was the best in the city; and Nashville was always celebrated as one of the most thriving and prosperous cities in the South. Hotel-keeping was not suffering, like other trading concerns, from the depression of the moment. This hotel was crammed with guests, and had been crammed throughout the previous winter. Outside it was handsome enough, but internally, I say without hesitation, it was the dirtiest and worst managed hotel it had been ever my fortune to stop at. The dirt was dirt of old standing, and the mismanagement must have been the growth of years long preceding the days when secession was first heard of. The bar, as I mentioned, was closed by order; but the *habitués* still hung about the scene of their former pleasures. In the hall there were a number of broken shattered chairs, and here, with their legs stretched in every conceivable position, a number of well-dressed respectable-looking persons used to loaf all day long, smoking and chewing. They did not seem to have anything to do, or much to say to each other; but they sat there to kill time by looking at one another. The floor was as dirty as successive strata of tobacco-juice could make it; and, at the slightest symptom of chill in the air, the stove was kindled to a red-hot heat, and the atmosphere was made as stifling as the cracks in the doors would permit it to become. The passages were as filthy as want of sweeping could make them; and dirty cloths, slop-pails, and brooms were left lying about them, all day and every day; the narrow wooden staircases were such as you would hardly see in England leading to the poorest of attics; and the household arrangements were as primitive as was consistent with the dirtiness peculiar to civilized life. As to the meals, their profusion was only equalled by their greasiness, and by the utter nondescriptness of their component victuals. The chicken-pie tasted uncommonly like the stewed mutton, and both were equally unlike any compound I ever ate before. I could understand why it was thought unnecessary for the negroes to waste soap and water on washing; but the same reason could not apply to their jackets and shirts, which I presume once were white. The servants were all negroes, and all, naturally enough, devoted their minds to doing as little work and taking as long about it as possible. What seemed more odd than all, none of the habitual residents—some of them persons of property—appeared to be aware that the establishment was dirty and uncomfortable. The heat of the house must have been fearful in summer and the smells pestilential; for, with a southern climate, the style of building maintained was that of the small rooms and narrow passages of England. Nor was this a single instance. The other hotels in the city were worse; and some of my friends who have travelled through the Southern States have assured me that, except in the very large towns, the hotels are invariably of the same description. The truth is, that where the whites think it beneath them to work, and where the negroes will not work unless they are forced, you cannot expect domestic comfort.

THE BATTLE OF CHICKAMAUGA

SEPTEMBER 19-20, 1863

Source: America. <u>Great Crises In Our History Told By Its Makers</u>. Chicago: Issued by Americanization Department, Veterans of Foreign Wars of the United States, 1925.

By Brigadier-General George H. Thomas

IT was as commander of the left wing of the Union army at Chickamauga, Tennessee (September 19-20, 1863), that General Thomas, who made this official report to the War Department, displayed such courage and military genius as to save the Union army from overwhelming defeat, and earn for himself the title of "The Rock of Chickamauga." In this sanguinary engagement the Union and Confederate losses were about 34,000 in killed, wounded and missing, about equally divided. Opposing 55,000 Federal troops was a Confederate army of about 70,000. Though the battle was won by the Confederates, under General Bragg, the prize for which it was fought, the city of Chattanooga, remained in possession of the Federals, under Rosecrans.

This account begins on September 18, and pictures the eventful September 20, when the Federals were routed, leaving Thomas to stand firm against tremendous odds, before retiring under cover of darkness.

AT 4 p. m. the whole corps moved to the left along Chickamauga Creek to Crawfish Spring. On arriving at that place received orders to march on the cross-road leading by Widow Glenn's house to the Chattanooga and La Fayette road, and take up a position near Kelly's farm, on the La Fayette road, connecting with Crittenden on my right at Gordon's Mills. The head of the column reached Kelly's farm about daylight on the 19th [September, 1863] Baird's division in front, and took up a position at the forks of the road, facing toward Reed's and Alexander's Bridges over the Chickamauga. Colonel Wilder, commanding the mounted brigade of Reynolds' division, informed me that the enemy had crossed the Chickamauga in force at those two bridges the evening before and drove his brigade across the State road, or Chattanooga and La Fayette road, to the heights east of Widow Glenn's house.

Kelly's house is situated in an opening about three-fourths of a mile long and one-fourth of a mile wide, on the east side of the State road, and stretches along that road in a northerly direction, with a small field of perhaps 20 acres on the west side of the road, directly opposite to the house. From thence to the Chickamauga the surface of the country is undulating and covered with original forest timber, interspersed with undergrowth, in many places so dense that it is difficult to see 50 paces ahead. There is a cleared field near Jay's Mill, and cleared land in the vicinity of Reed's and Alexander's Bridges. A narrow field commences at a point about a fourth of a mile south of Kelly's house, on the east side of the State road, and extends, perhaps, for half a mile along the road toward Gordon's Mills. Between the State road and the foot of Missionary Ridge there is a skirt of timber stretching from the vicinity of Widow Glenn's house, south of the forks of the road to McDonald's house, three-fourths of a mile north of Kelly's. The eastern slope of the Missionary Ridge, between Glenn's and McDonald's, is cleared and mostly under cultivation. This position of Baird's threw my right in close proximity to Wilder's brigade; the interval I intended to fill up with the two remaining brigades of Reynolds' division on their arrival. General Brannan, closely following Baird's division, was placed in position on his left, on the two roads leading from the State road to Reed's and Alexander's Bridges.

Colonel Dan. McCook, commanding a brigade of the Reserve Corps, met me at General Baird's headquarters, and reported to me that he had been stationed the previous night on the road leading to Reed's Bridge, and that he could discover no force of the enemy except one brigade, which had crossed to the west side of the Chickamauga at Reed's Bridge the day before; and he believed it could be cut off, because, after it had crossed, he had destroyed the bridge, the enemy having retired toward Alexander's Bridge. Upon this information I directed General Brannan to post a brigade, within supporting distance of Baird, on the road to Alexander's Bridge, and with his other two brigades to reconnoiter the road leading to Reed's Bridge to see if he could locate the brigade reported by Colonel McCook, and, if a favorable opportunity occurred, to capture it. His dispositions were made according to instructions by 9 a. m.

General Baird was directed to throw forward his right wing, so as to get more nearly in line with Brannan, but to watch well on his right flank. Soon after this disposition of those two divisions, a portion of Palmer's division, of Crittenden's corps, took position to the right of General Baird's division. About

10 o'clock Croxton's brigade of Brannan's division, posted on the road leading to Alexander's Bridge, became engaged with the enemy, and I rode forward to his position to ascertain the character of the attack. Colonel Croxton reported to me that he had driven the enemy nearly half a mile, but that he was then meeting with obstinate resistance. I then rode back to Baird's position, and directed him to advance to Croxton's support, which he did with his whole division, Starkweather's brigade in reserve, and drove the enemy steadily before him for some distance, taking many prisoners. Croxton's brigade, which had been heavily engaged for over an hour with greatly superior numbers of the enemy, and being nearly exhausted of ammunition, was then moved to the rear to enable the men to fill up their boxes; and Baird and Brannan, having united their forces, drove the enemy from their immediate front. General Baird then halted for the purpose of readjusting his line; and hearing from prisoners that the enemy were in heavy force on his immediate right, he threw back his right wing in order to be ready for an attack from that quarter.

Before his dispositions could be completed, the enemy, in overwhelming numbers, furiously assaulted Scribner's and King's brigades, and drove them in disorder. Fortunately, at this time Johnson's division, of McCook's corps, and Reynolds' division, of my corps, arrived, and were immediately placed in position. Johnson preceded Reynolds, his left connecting with Baird's right, and Palmer being immediately on Johnson's right, Reynolds was placed on the right of Palmer, with one brigade of his division in reserve. As soon as formed they advanced upon the enemy, attacking him in flank and driving him in great disorder for a mile and a half, while Brannan's troops met him in front as he was pursuing Baird's retiring brigades, driving the head of his column back and retaking the artillery, which had been temporarily lost by Baird's brigades, the Ninth Ohio recovering Battery H, Fifth U. S. Artillery, at the point of the bayonet. The enemy, at this time being hardly pressed by Johnson, Palmer, and Reynolds in flank, fell back in confusion upon his reserves, posted in a strong position on the west side of Chickamauga Creek between Reed's and Alexander's Bridges.

Brannan and Baird were then ordered to reorganize their commands and take position on commanding ground on the road from McDonald's to Reed's Bridge, and hold it to the last extremity, as I expected the next effort of the enemy would be to gain that road and our rear. This was about 2 p. m. After a lull of about one hour, a furious attack was made upon Reynolds' right, and he having called upon me for re-enforcements, I directed Brannan's division to move to his support, leaving King's brigade, of Baird's division, to hold the position at which Baird and Brannan had been posted, the balance of Baird's division closing up to the right on Johnson's division. . . .

Before adjusting the line satisfactorily, I received an order to report to department headquarters immediately, and was absent from my command until near midnight. After my return from department headquarters, about 2 a. m. on the 20th, I received a report from General Baird that the left of his division did not rest on the Reed's Bridge road, as I had intended, and that he could not reach it without weakening his line too much. I immediately addressed a note to the general commanding requesting that General Negley be sent me to take position on Baird's left and rear, and thus secure our left from assault. During the night the troops threw up temporary breastworks of logs, and prepared for the encounter which all anticipated would come off the next day.

Although informed by note, from General Rosecrans' headquarters, that Negley's division would be sent immediately to take post on my left, it had not arrived at 7 a. m. on the 20th, and I sent Captain Willard, of my staff, to General Negley to urge him forward as rapidly as possible, and to point out his position to him. General Negley, in his official report, mentions that he received this order through Captain Willard at 8 a. m. on the 20th, and that he immediately commenced withdrawing his division for that purpose, when the enemy was reported to be massing a heavy force in his front, sharply engaging his skirmishers, and that he was directed by General Rosencrans to hold his position until relieved by some other command. General Beatty's brigade, however, was sent under the guidance of Captain Willard, who took it to its position, and it went into action immediately. The enemy at that time commenced a furious assault on Baird's left, and partially succeeded in gaining his rear. . . .

To prevent a repetition of this attack of the enemy on our left I directed Captain Gaw, chief topographical officer on my staff, to go to the commanding officer of the troops on the left and rear of Baird, and direct him to mass as much artillery on the slopes of Missionary Ridge, west of the State road, as he could conveniently spare from his lines, supported strongly by infantry, so as to sweep the ground to the left and rear of Baird's position. . . .

General Wood barely had time to dispose his troops on the left of Brannan before another of those fierce assaults, similar to those made in the morning on my lines, was made on him and Brannan combined, and kept up by the enemy throwing in fresh troops as fast as those in their front were driven back, until near nightfall. About the time that Wood took up his position, General Gordon Granger appeared on my left flank at the head of Steedman's division of his corps. I immediately dispatched a staff officer, Captain Johnson, Second Indiana Cavalry, of Negley's division, to him with orders to push forward and take position on Brannan's right, which order was complied with with the greatest promptness and alacrity. Steedman, moving his division into position with almost as much precision as if on drill, and fighting his wey to the crest of the hill on Brannan's right, moved forward his artillery and drove the enemy down the southern slope, inflicting on him a most terrible loss in killed and wounded. This opportune arrival of fresh troops revived the flagging spirits of our men on the right, and inspired them with new ardor for the contest. Every assault of the enemy from that time until nightfall was repulsed in the most gallant style by the whole line.

By this time the ammunition in the boxes of the men was reduced, on an average, to 2 or 3 rounds per man, and my ammunition trains having been unfortunately ordered to the rear by some unauthorized person, we should have been entirely without ammunition in a very short time had not a small supply come up with General Steedman's command. This, being distributed among the troops, gave them about 10 rounds per man.

General Garfield, chief of staff of General Rosecrans, reached this position about 4 p. m., in company with Lieutenant-Colonel Thruston, of McCook's staff, and Captains Gaw and Barker, of my staff, who had been sent to the rear to bring back the ammunition, if possible. General Garfield gave me the first reliable information that the right and center of our army had been driven, and of its condition at that time. I soon after received a dispatch from General Rosecrans, directing me to assume command of all the forces, and, with Crittenden and McCook, take a strong position and assume a threatening attitude at Rossville, sending the unorganized forces to Chattanooga for reorganization, stating that he would examine the ground at Chattanooga, and then join me; also that he had sent out rations and ammunition to meet me at Rossville.

I determined to hold the position until nightfall, if possible, in the meantime sending Captains Barker and Kellogg to distribute the ammunition, Major Lawrence, my chief of artillery, having been previously sent to notify the different commanders that ammunition would be supplied them shortly. As soon as they reported the distribution of the ammunition, I directed Captain Willard to inform the division commanders to prepare to withdraw their commands as soon as they received orders. At 5.30 p.m. Captain Barker, commanding my escort, was sent to notify General Reynolds to commence the movement, and I left the position behind General Wood's command to meet Reynolds and point out to him the position where I wished him to form line to cover the retirement of the other troops on the left.

In passing through an open woods bordering the State road, and between my last and Reynolds' position, I was cautioned by a couple of soldiers, who had been to hunt water, that there was a large force of the rebels in these woods, drawn up in line and advancing toward me. Just at this time I saw the head of Reynolds' column approaching, and calling to the general himself, directed him to form line perpendicular to the State road, changing the head of his column to the left, with his right resting on that road, and to charge the enemy, who were then in his immediate front. This movement was made with the utmost promptitude, and facing to the right while on the march, Turchin threw his brigade upon the rebel force, routing them and driving them in utter confusion entirely beyond Baird's left. In this splendid advance more than 200 prisoners were captured and sent to the rear. . . . I then proceeded to Rossville, accompanied by Generals Garfield and Gordon Granger, and immediately prepared to place the troops in position at that point. One brigade of Negley's division was posted in the gap, on the Ringgold road, and two brigades on the top of the ridge to the right of the road, adjoining the brigade in the road; Reynolds' division on the right of Negley's and reaching to the Dry Valley road; Brannan's division in the rear of Reynolds' right, as a reserve; McCook's corps on the right of the Dry Valley road, and stretching toward the west, his right reaching nearly to Chattanooga Creek; Crittenden's entire corps was posted on the heights to the left of the Ringgold road, with Steedman's division of Granger's corps in reserve behind his left; Baird's division in reserve, and in supporting distance of the brigade in the gap; McCook's brigade of Granger's corps was also posted as a reserve to the brigade of Negley on the top of the ridge, to the right of the road; Minty's brigade of cavalry was on the Ringgold road, about a mile and a half in advance of the gap.

About 10 a. m. of the 21st, receiving a message from Minty that the enemy were advancing on him with a strong force of cavalry and infantry, I directed him to retire through the gap and post his command on our left flank, and throw out strong reconnoitering parties across the ridge to observe and report any movements of the enemy on our left front. From information received from citizens, I was convinced that the position was untenable in the face of the odds we had opposed to us, as the enemy could easily concentrate upon our right flank, which, if driven, would expose our center and left to be entirely cut off from our communications. I therefore advised the commanding general to concentrate the troops at Chattanooga. About the time I made the suggestion to withdraw, the enemy made a demonstration on the direct road, but were soon repulsed. In anticipation of this order to concentrate at Chattanoga, I sent for the corps commanders, and gave such general instructions as would enable them to prepare their commands for making the movement without confusion. All wagons, ambulances, and surplus artillery carriages were sent to the rear before night.

The order for the withdrawal being received about 6 p. m. the movement commenced at 9 p. m., in the following order: Strong skirmish lines, under the direction of judicious officers, were thrown out to the front of each division to cover this movement, with directions to retire at daylight, deployed and in supporting distance, the whole to be supported by the First Division, Fourteenth Army Corps, under the superintendence of Major-General Rousseau, assisted by Minty's brigade of cavalry, which was to follow after the skirmishers. Crittenden's corps was to move from the hill to the left of the road at 9 p. m., followed by Steedman's division. Next Negley's division was to withdraw at 10 p. m.; then Reynolds, McCook's corps, by divisions from left to right, moving within supporting distance one after the other; Brannan's division was posted at 6 p. m. on the road about half way between Rossville and Chattanooga to cover the movement. The troops were withdrawn in a quiet, orderly manner, without the loss of a single man, and by 7 a. m. on the 22d were in their positions in front of Chattanooga, which had been assigned to them previous to their arrival, and which they now occupy, covered by strong intrenchments thrown up on the day of our arrival, and strengthened from day to day until they were considered sufficiently strong for all defensive purposes.

COTTON PATCH LIFE IN TENNESSEE

This is an interesting picture of Tennessee life, people and customs during the early 20th century.

Source: Clifton Johnson. <u>Highways and Byways of the Mississippi Valley</u>. New York: The Macmillan Company, 1906, 84-105.

I WAS only a short distance from Memphis, yet the region was almost as raw and rustic as if there had not been a large town within a hundred miles. To be sure great fields of corn and cotton were numerous; but I did not have to go far to strike the forest, and only a few decades have passed since the woodland was nearly omnipresent. The trees have been laid low to make fence rails and railroad ties, and to supply fuel for the old, wood-burning locomotives. Much of what was cut was ruthlessly wasted or sold for a song. "If the timber was standing now that was hyar twenty years ago," said one man, "we'd all make our fortunes handling it. Why, I've chopped down a coon tree and let it lie and rot that'd be worth forty dollars to-day."

The spring was backward, but the corn had been planted and was beginning to come up, and the cotton fields had been ploughed and ridged and much of the seed was in. On my first day, work was pretty much at a standstill, for a heavy rain the previous night had converted the fields into mud and bog.

I started out for a ramble, and as long as I kept to the "pike" the travelling was fairly good; but as soon as I turned off on to a dirt road I was in sticky red clay, and had to pick my route with caution. There were more blacks than whites in this region, and the country was dotted over with their cabins. Many of the huts were made of logs, and they were all primitive. Some were so rudely constructed, and so open to the onsets of the storms, you wondered how they could be used for dwellings. The old lanes along which these homes were scattered were very wild and picturesque. There were stumps in them and occasional large trees, while along the fences grew briers and bushes. Frequently they were hardly more than a cart track wide, and were so rough and rutted as to be practically impassable for a Christian vehicle. In explanation of the badness of these byways, I was told that only negroes lived along them; and that therefore the local authorities never troubled themselves to "work" the roads. "Dey think anything will do fo' colored folks," was one negro's comment.

A rural delivery route ran through the district, and nearly every dwelling had its metal box set out by the roadside on a post. The white people owned their boxes at a cost of a dollar and thirty cents; but they told me that the negroes mostly rented theirs from a Memphis daily newspaper, and paid sixty-five cents a month for box and paper. A representative of the paper had explained to the negroes that they could not have boxes except on these conditions, and that if they were without a box they could only get their mail by going to Memphis for it. Many of them did not want the paper and could not afford the expense, but they were too inexperienced to comprehend the swindle or to know what to do about it. The colored families are apt to take a religious weekly, and every negro has thoughts and opinions on the topics of the time, especially on those that affect his own race; but, as one of them said, "Hit doan' do to talk much or we git into a heap er trouble. We low-born, an' the white folks are not likin' us to say anything."

The commonest type of negro home in the neighborhood was a long, single-story structure, with a kitchen at one end and sleeping apartments at the other, and an open passage-way between, known as "the entry." This entry served to separate the heated kitchen from the rest of the dwelling, and was a combination of porch, shed, and open-sided room for work and loitering. Its walls and roof made a handy hanging-place for all sorts of articles. The chimneys were outside at the ends of the house. They were usually of wooden slats thickly bedaubed with a mixture of clay and dry grass. "De clay an' grass chimney ain' ve'y endurable," I was informed, "an' in about fo' years dey have to be built over."

Toward noon I passed through a long stretch of woodland. Off among the trees I could hear the ding-dong of cowbells, the cooing of turtle-doves, the drum-beat of the "peckerwoods," and the trilling and twittering and whistling of a multitude of other birds. The wind rustled softly through the new foliage and the air was permeated with the odors of spring. Here and there were dashes of dogwood bloom, and patches of May-apple were coming into flower on the ground. I stopped for dinner at a farmhouse. The place was a half-wild sort of a ranch, the house badly out of repair, and in the home yard roamed numbers of turkeys, ducks, hens, goats, and hogs. Two of the older girls had been busy that morning picking up the dry last year's stalks in the corn field and piling them to burn. One of the boys, about ten years old, had been ploughing with a mule.

We ate in the hot and grimy kitchen. Pork and mustard greens, corn-bread and coffee, were chief on the bill of fare. The farmer suggested I might prefer milk instead of coffee, and he poured a glass for me; but one taste was enough. The children of the family drank it freely, and the man also took a tumblerful. As he finished it he casually remarked that the milk was a little sour. I wondered that he said "a little," for it was half curdled.

He entertained me very handsomely and exemplified what he called "the old-fashioned Southern hospitality," that was "glad to see you come, and sorry to see you go." He observed further, that "Befo' the war nothing gave a man more pleasure than to do honor to his guest. You were treated with special respect, even at the hotels. Why, I used to know a landlord who, after a man registered, always wrote in front of the signature 'Capt.,' 'Maj.,' or 'Col.,' so that no one stopping at his hotel failed to have a military title. He was a genuine polished old-style gentleman, and his guests was all treated like they was persons of distinction."

My host said he was going fishing later in the day. "This is just the right time of year for it," he declared.

"'Dogwood white
Fisher's delight,'

you know. Every old colored woman gets her hook

and line ready when the dogwood blossoms, and so do all the rest of us."

By night, when I returned to my boarding-place, the weather had turned cold, and the next day was so chilly and clouded I stayed indoors most of the time. A rude wind buffeted the trees and soughed wearily about the house, and I sat beside the kitchen fireplace to enjoy the grateful heat of the brisk fire that was kept burning there. The gloomy skies and the bleak and boisterous wind seemed to put my landlady in a mood for telling ghost stories. "The first thing I remember of my childhood," said she, "is of sitting out on the porch of a moonlight night and hearing the darkies tell about the witches. When I went to bed I was so scared thinking a witch might come through the keyhole, I jus' couldn't sleep.

"The niggers have a lot of queer ways. They take poisonous snakes' heads and pound 'em up with other poisonous things to put in hoodoo bags; and then they hide the bags under the doorstep, or in the bed of the person they want to harm. Once I was sick for a long time and no one could make out what the trouble was. At last the house burned and most everything in it; but we saved my feather bed, and I tore it up to make pillows. Inside I found a hoodoo ring made of feathers twisted into a band or ring fifteen inches across, and tied to it was a hundred or more little bags. I put it in the fire, and after that I got well. I 'spose I'd been inhalin' the poison.

"When you was in Memphis did you see Brinkley Hall? I went to school there. Well, one night my room-mate and me was sitting together with a lighted lamp on our table. Suddenly some one blew out the light, and the lamp chimney went on the floor and was smashed. We was all in darkness, and we ran to the door. It was a door that never would close tight; but it was tight shut now and we couldn't get out. We heard some one walking in the room over the broken glass of the lamp chimney, and we began to scream. The girls in the rooms near us came to our door, and we told them what had happened, and how we couldn't get out. They laughed at us, but when they listened and heard the footsteps they went to shrieking. That brought the principal running up the stairs, and he opened the door; but there was nothing to see only some broken glass on the floor and us two girls limp with fright.

"After that all sorts of things happened at the school. The girls used to hear the noise of water falling on the floor, and bells would ring with no one ringing them; and there was one scholar named Flora Robinson who would go into a trance, and see a little girl in a pale pink dress who kept following her. Once the little girl had her take a pencil and write, and the writing said that if Flora's folks would dig in a certain place they'd find jars with papers in 'em showing that Brinkley Hall belonged to the Robinsons. So her folks got some men to dig in that place, and a few feet down they came to a brick wall, and they tore that to pieces and found three glass jars, and they could see money and papers inside. They decided to let the jars stay right there till next day when they would open 'em before proper authorities. A man stood guard; but during the night he was knocked on the head, and the jars was stolen. So much had happened that the school broke up, and Brinkley Hall with its forty rooms is vacant yet.

"Another strange thing in my own experience happened after my husband died. He was very fond of music, and in his last sickness he said if he could return to earth he would make his presence known by playing the piano. One day just at supper time, after he'd been dead about two weeks, I heard the piano play. All the children heard it, too, and we jumped up from the table, scared to death. I said I never would want to use that piano again, and I sent it to Memphis to be sold."

My landlady in concluding urged me to call on a negro family by the name of Houston that lived next door and ask them what they knew about witches and other occult things. Their house was in a yard full of trees, and its aspect was rather pleasant from a distance, but when I got a close view I found it was shabby and decrepit. I was welcomed into the kitchen, a dismal place that gloomy day in spite of the flames flickering in the fireplace. The floor sagged dubiously, the ceiling was brown with smoke, and panes were missing from the windows, and the holes stuffed with rags. Newspapers were pasted in a queer motley over the walls. The room had two beds. On one of them lay a gun. A sick girl was in the other, and the rest of the family sat in a circle at the borders of the rough, deepworn hearth doing very little except to spit into the fire at frequent intervals. Mrs. Houston and her two daughters each had a wad of snuff inside of her under lip. My landlady had mentioned that a pedler of spectacles had recently been along. "He had two qualities," said she, "one for white folks at a dollar and a half, and one for darkies, with brass bows, at seventy-five cents. Houston bought a pair for himself, and a pair for the old woman. He wanted his oldest girl to have a pair, too, because they were fashionable, but she wouldn't."

Sure enough, when I entered the kitchen, Mr. Houston went to the window-sill and got his spectacles, and handed his wife hers, and they both put them on. We were soon talking about the mysteries, and Mr. Houston said: "De witches ride our horses at night. In de mornin' we'll find der manes and tails full of witches stirrups — de ha'r all twisted and tangled up. It couldn't twis' itself up dataway, an' yo' cain't pick de ha'r straight in an hour. You have to cut it. You can lock yo' horses up an' tie 'em tight as yo' please; but it make no dif'runce, de witches git 'em an' use 'em jus' de same. Sometimes, too, de witches come in de house when you asleep an' ride *you*, an' you wake up all tired an' lame."

"I doan' min' de witches so much as de conjurations," remarked Mrs. Houston.

"Well," said the man, "if yo' find a conjure thing, all yo' got to do is to put some silver money in yo' shoes, an' you c'n walk over it widout gittin' any harm."

"But it ain' often yo' find it befo' hand," she objected, "an' I doan' want to keep money in my shoes all de time."

"My oldes' girl, Em'line, was tricked once," the man went on. "She'd have a pain in her breast, an' nex' minute de pain would be in her side, an' den in her back — de pain keep movin' aroun' all over her an' was worryin' her to death. We went after a medical doctor, and when he see her he turn white an' scratch his haid an' look like he scared. He did de bes' he could fo' her, but ev'y bit er de medicine what he give her she throwed up. We tried some mo' doctors, an' dey ev'y one give her a round er medicine; but none of 'em couldn't help her. She had spells like she was dyin' an' got black under her eyes an' round her lips, an' she said it no use to sen' fo' any one else. But we went an' got a hoodoo doctor from Memphis. Soon as he come he say to her, 'Who you shuck hands wid?'

"She tol' him she ain't shuck hands wid nobody; but he say some one had hol' er her hand shore, an' he describe de man, an' she know who de man is. He a feller what been wantin' to marry her. We try to raise our children nice an' 'spectable, an' we want 'em to keep de bes' company dar is, an' dat feller too no account. So she wouldn't have him. She say she ain't shuck hands wid him; but one day she climbin' up a bank, an' dat man had caught her by de arm an' holp her up, an' no sooner did he do dat dan she fin' herse'f havin' de trembles. De hoodoo doctor he listen an' lif' his eyebrows; but he 'pear not to be sati'fied yit. He look aroun',' an' he say, 'Dar somethin' bad in dis hyar house;' an' he ask Em'line, 'Whar dose pillows on yo' bed been to?'

"Den he took 'em an' rip 'em open, an' dar was a conjure thing big as yo' fis' in each one. It was a piece er cloth wid wax on both sides, an' all kind er feathers quirled aroun' and aroun' in de wax. De hoodoo doctor pass one to me, but when I took it in my han' a cramp run plumb up in my shoulder. I couldn't hol' it. Nex' thing, de doctor look at de bottles er medicine on de table, an' set 'em all aside, an' tol' us not to use 'em no mo'. Den he give Em'line a little shot er quicksilver an' she swallow it an' was cured. I done heard that quicksilver is death fo' a well person to take any of it; but if yo' been conjured it ketch de pizen an' doan' hurt yo' none."

"Yo' c'n tell whether yo' been tricked," said Mrs. Houston, "by takin' a piece er silver money an' sleepin' wid it in yo' mouth. If yo' been conjured, de silver, in de mornin', be jus' as black as a coal wid spots er yaller like copper on it."

"De hoodoo doctor charge ten dollars fo' what he done," Mr. Houston resumed. "Dat a heap to pay, an' yit, if I was took sick bad, I shore would send fo' him."

"De same feller what trick Em'line made de attemp' atterward to conjure de whole chu'ch," said Mrs. Houston.

"Yes," observed Mr. Houston, "I see him put a little mess under de chu'ch doorstep an' bury it. I didn't know certain what he doin', but I step aroun' it when I went in. Yuthers, dey step over it, an' dey git conjured. Our preacher man, he git conjured, too, an' no sooner is he preachin' dan he make out like he mighty happy, an' he put his arms round de sisters an' hugged 'em. I reckon if he hadn't been wearin' a silver watch which kind er protect him, he'd been killed. My nephew was took sick at de same time right dar in meetin', an' I tol' him what de matter was. So he jump on a mule an' rode as fas' as he could to de doctor to git himself worked on. Atter meetin' I took a stick an' pull de conjure thing out from under de doorstep, an' de nex' Sunday we discuss de matter in de chu'ch to see what we better do about de feller; but he had skipped, an' he ain' been round hyar since."

"I mighty glad he gone, too," Mrs. Houston commented. "De way he done trick Em'line give me de worst scare I had since freedom. Yas, dat de bigges' shakeup I ever expe'ence, excep' in de war when dey had a battle near whar I lived. Oh, my Lord, how dey fought! We'd hear de guns a-firin' fast as dey could pop, an' once in a while a big cannon would bang. De Southern soldiers went marchin' past, back an' forth, an' dey go all through people's fields. Lord 'a' mercy! dey'd throw down de fences dat was in de way, an' make a wide dusty road right through de green fields. Den de Northern soldiers come, thousands an' millions of 'em, I reckon, an' dey took all our horses an' mules, an' all de hams out er our smoke-houses. Some er de white folks would hide der things, but de Northern soldiers would git hol' er de darkies an' threaten to kill 'em if dey didn't tell whar de things was. Dey begun to build forts, an' dey tell de planters to sen' der darkies to help. One mighty mean man said he wa'n't gwine have his darkies workin' fo' de North. So dey took his two sons an' put dem at diggin'. Dat make him think he made a mistake, an' he didn't was'e no time in bringin' de darkies to take his sons' place."

"I holped de Republican party build dem breastworks," declared Mr. Houston. "Dat de fust work I done fo' de Republican party. It wa'n't long befo' de Rebs had been run out from aroun' hyar. De cars kep' comin' all de time loaded inside an' outside wid Republican party soldiers, an' in der uniforms dey look jus' like bluebirds. Some colored men jine de Republican party army an' went to fight, an' dey want me go too; but I'd got a wife, an' I didn't want to be separate from her an' perhaps never see her again. Besides, I didn't know whether de North gwine beat, though it look mo' bad fo' de South all de time. Yit I kep' out er de army way to de end, becaze I reckoned if de Republican party win, I be free whedder I fight or not. If she git licked I better not be too much mix up in de rumpus."

Back of the village to the east was a wide expanse of corn and cotton fields extending over to some woods along a creek. Bordering the woods were frequent cabins, and these were connected with the village by irregular paths skirting the ditches and edges of the fields and occasionally taking a straight cut across the cultivated grounds. Most of this land rented for five dollars an acre. Corn and cotton were the chief crops, but some of it was planted to potatoes and pease. In good weather the region is very busy with men, women, and children intent on earning the money to pay the rent and get a living for themseves. They begin to put in the cotton seed when the scrub hickory buds; and a white man told me that negroes depended so much on nature thus to indicate the proper time, that "If the scrub hickory didn't never bud they wouldn't never expect to plant."

A month later the cotton is ready for its first "chopping" — that is, hoeing. They start picking in September, and money is then more plentiful than at any other season. Most of the negroes, in addition to caring for their own crops, do a good deal of picking for the whites. The pay is fifty to seventy-five cents a hundred, and the day's labor begins as soon as the dew dries and ends a half hour before sunset. "It's fun to any one to pick cotton," an old woman said to me. "I've picked over two hundred in a day many a time, and nursed my baby and milked my cow and cooked dinner fo' me an' my ole man an' three chillen. De men de bes' pickers. Some of 'em certainly can snatch it. De women gits tired in de back, an' de men dey hol' out longer. When dere's a prize offered I seen men pick much as four hundred pounds er dis yer big boll cotton in one day."

The fields are at their whitest just after the first frosts. Then all the bolls open and the cotton patches look as if there had been a fall of snow. The frost also loosens the cotton and makes picking easy. The work goes on for many weeks, and there is some desultory gleaning all through the winter. One famous cotton picker is "Uncle Henry," reputed to be over a hundred years old. He never cuts his finger nails, because he wants them to grow long, so he can have their aid in getting the cotton quickly out of the bolls. I called on him one day at his house, and as I approached I heard him singing a curious negro hymn.

> "A gospel hook got-a-hung to my heart,
> Eli shoutin' in de heaven, 'Good Lord!
> Good Lord! Good Lord!'
> Eli shoutin' in de heaven, 'Good Lord!'"

His home was on the edge of the woods, a whitewashed log dwelling with a huddle of little outbuildings and fenced enclosures roundabout. Uncle Henry was sitting by the kitchen fire entertaining several grandchildren. The grizzled old negro looked to be about fourscore; but he had no doubt he was entitled to thirty years more, and said there were lots of colored people one hundred and twenty and one hundred and twenty-five years of age. He remembered distinctly the "falling of the stars" in 1833, and any negro whose memory has that span is a patriarch of his race. Aside from the war, that is the greatest event of modern times in the chronicles of the colored folks.

"I was about ten years ole, I reckon," said Uncle Henry, "and I was out playin' hide and coop wid a parcel er white boys, an' we thought it was a snowstorm at de start. Den, de fust news I knew my mammy an' missis was a-hollerin' an' cryin', 'Lord have mercy! Lord have mercy!' an' sayin' it was de end er de worl'. My missis made noise enough, I can tell yo' dat. I never heared such a voice as dat woman had. One er our men was name Dave Tucker, an' he was de only man on de place what could hive bees. When de bees swarmed he bleeged to come, an' my ole missis could holler an' call him from five miles away.

"Dat night I speakin' about it appear like ev'y star in de sky was a-fallin'. Some er de boys try to cotch 'em in der hats, but de stars go out befo' dey git to de groun'. Dey lit up de whole earth, an' as dey fell dey made a sissin' soun' like de soun' er draps er water thrown on a hot skillet. My oldes' brudder, he'd been out 'mongst de gals dat night, an' he was on his journey home when he heard de roarin' er de stars a-fallin', an' he thought de whole elements was burnin' an' de judgment come. He reckoned his time was out, an' de got down den an' dar on his knees an' he prayed, 'O Lord, come quickly, come quickly, I greatly need yo'!'

"Dem dat hadn't never prayed in der lives prayed a li'l' bit dat night, an' I hear tell er one man — an' he was a ve'y ole man too — he ain' been use to prayin', an' he try to say de Lord's Prayer; but when he git to, 'Thy kingdom come, thy will be done,' he kind er mixed, an' he say instead, 'Lord, kick 'em as dey come!' Yas, it scare us all, an' in less'n two weeks ev'ybody, white an' black, got religion. Dar was mo' religion dan enough."

When I left Uncle Henry one of his grandsons became my guide on the uncertain paths that linked cabin to cabin and connected them with the village. He told me about a gun he had, and how he had shot rabbits and tried to shoot ducks.

"What's that bird we hear in the tall trees just ahead?" I interrupted.

"Dat's a kind er a li'l' ole bird call' a wren," was the reply.

Then he pointed out a redbird and some "jay birds," and said, "De redbird de prettiest bird we got. Dar's lots er birds hyar — peckerwoods an' sapsuckers an' yallerhammers an' robins; an' dar's de rain crows what set up in de trees an' holler when it's fixin' for to rain; an' a li'l' ole speckle bird call a thrush. Some er de birds are good to eat, an' in de winter time I knock 'em down wid a stick. Dey roun' stumps atter something to feed on, an' it so col' dey won't hardly fly. Yo' be astonish' how col' it is hyar sometimes; but in summer, it often so hot we cain't scarcely stay in our clothes. We gwine along de bottoms near de crick now. Yo' hear all dat hollerin' over dar? Dat de spring frogs. Dey a li'l' muddy color frog no bigger dan de end er my thumb. Dey de firs' frog in de spring. De toad frog an' de bullfrog doan' come until it git right warm."

The boy was surprisingly keen in his knowledge of the little creatures of the fields and woods. He was himself a child of nature, a companion of the wild, whose world was narrow, but not by any means uninteresting. Nor was he at all unusual. Most of the blacks are well versed in this sort of lore, and in a simple way the field, the forest, and the air serve them for the information and entertainment which most of us go to books to gain.

The labor of the families who depended on the cotton patches for a living did not seem to me to yield very satisfactory returns. Few are able to attain a safe prosperity, and poverty stalks along behind most, ever threatening to drag them off their little holdings. Such conditions were often revealed to me by my chance acquaintances. For instance, I one day stopped a negro who was driving a farm cart through the spring mud of the highway and asked directions. While we were talking a colored woman came plodding along and spoke to the man. "Hit been a long time since I seen you, Brother Bealy," said she. "How yo' gittin' on?"

"Well," he replied, "I had a hard expe'ence dis las' winter wid de rheumatism; but hit has let up on me some now."

"Yo' luck sholy have been bad, Brother Bealy," said the woman sympathetically.

"I done met some heavy ole jars, Sister Larkin," he admitted. "Las' year de secon' time I been sol' out on account er mortgages. Hit quite a th'owback for me. I got six chillen an' a wife a-swingin' on top er me, an' hit no easy matter to pay my rent and all de yuther expenses."

"Yas, to take keer er yo' fambly, yo' oblige to hit hard an' often," was the woman's comment; "but if yo' keep up heart, de Lord, He boun' to pull you through."

The man removed his hat and rubbed his head thoughtfully. "I gwine to stick to my work long as I c'n move," he said; "and I'm gwine to pay all my honest debts from a nickel up. God knows I am."

"Dat right, Brother," the woman responded heartily, "an' doan' let any mo' mortgage be put on yo'. Dar's a heap er people you an' me have knowed roun' hyar have got in debt till dey owed two or three hundred dollars, an' den dey so discourage dey lef' de country. Dese lenders keep puttin' on per cent and per cent, an' hit jus' nacherly ruins dem dey lends to."

"Yes," agreed the man, "fifteen per cent and ten

per cent and de principal, too, been mo' dan a good many could stan' under. Dey done all dey could, an' at las' dey give up ev'ything but de shirt on der back, an' some of 'em pull dat off an' say, 'Hyar, take dat too.'"

The man gathered up his reins preparing to drive on. "We been havin' pretty tolerable rough weather," said the woman.

"We certain have," was the man's response, "an' dat big win' las' night done shook my ole shack till I thought de house blow to pieces."

"Hit took off de las' er de apple bloom," the woman added, looking off over the landscape. "De trees look now like we have apples to bet on hyar mont' atter next."

"What yo' hear from yo' son in Texas, Sister Larkin?" asked the man.

"I plumb worried about him," she replied. "De las' news I heard he got de terrified fever."

They discussed this typhoid (?) fever, and then the man resumed his journey. I went on in company with the woman. She called my attention to the poor repair of the fences along the way, and told about "a no fence law" passed a few years before which obliged every one to keep their stock from running at large. Previously the crops had to be fenced, and the cattle and hogs were turned loose and went where they chose, and they "pretty nigh picked up der own livin'." But this wicked and incomprehensible law made it necessary to take care of them and feed them, and that didn't pay.

In concluding her remarks the woman philosophized thus: "Times have been; times will be; times wear out same like ev'ything else. De ways dey use to do ain' like de ways dey do now. Dese days, if yo' doan' take keer er yo' cattle dey're ketched an' yo' have to pay three or fo' dollars to git 'em ag'in."

The black cotton workers have their troubles, but they have their pleasures, too; and one of the chief of these pleasures is a debating society. This met every Saturday night in a spare room of a certain log cabin. The apartment was fitted up with a few benches and some boards laid on blocks, and it was pretty sure to be packed full. The discussions were very earnest and aroused much interest. "Las' Saturday," said a member of the society, "de question was, 'Which is de bes' beneficial, education or money?' Three fighted fo' education and three fighted fo' money, and education whooped. Anudder time we debate, 'Which has de deepes' effec' on a person's min', what he see, or what he hear?' Nex' time de question gwine be, 'Which done de mos' fo' de people — war or de ministry?'"

The negroes found delight in exercising their intellects at the debating society; but in the case of the whites, nothing appealed quite so strongly as the pleasure of satiating their stomachs at a barbecue. "Our barbecues are the biggest thing yet," I was told. "We most always have a neighborhood barbecue in August or September, and we have 'em at election speakin's, and Sunday-school picnics. When I was a boy we had one on the Fourth o' July. Everybody was bound to get done cultivating his corn and cotton by then so as to be ready to celebrate. Yes, you'd drive your mule till it didn't have any tail to get done by the Fourth. The way we fix for a barbecue is to begin to get ready the day befo'. The meat is roastin' all night. We have plenty of different meats — shoat, calf, kid, and goat, and we roast the whole animals. A trench is dug, and oak bark coals put in. Then sticks are laid across for the meat to rest on. Some white man has charge, but the niggers keep the fires goin' an' do the basting and the rough work.

"The next day everybody comes. There's a detail to do the carving, and we all step up and get what we want and go and sit down by some tree to eat it. Of course there's potatoes and cornmeal lightbread, and pickles and cake, and there's ice cream, and there's pure, genuine, strong coffee that the old ladies make, in abundance. Then there's fried chicken, if any one is fastidious enough to want it, and some enterprising fellow is likely to bring half a dozen bottles of beer and invite his special friends out to his buggy to drink it. But the best thing to my thinkin' is the shoat. A man hasn't got any part in the resurrection until he's eaten barbecued shoat."

The narrator's enthusiasm was quite superlative, and I have no doubt that the barbecues for the whites and the debating society for the blacks do much to brighten an otherwise somewhat sober existence.

BASIC FACTS

Capital City	Nashville
Nickname	The Volunteer State
Flower	Iris
Bird	Mockingbird
Tree	Tulip Poplar
Songs	*When It's Time in Tennessee;* and *The Tennessee Waltz*
Stone	Agate
Animal	Raccoon
Entered the Union	June 1, 1796

STATISTICS*

Land Area (square miles)	41,328
Rank in Nation	34th
Population†	4,072,000
Rank in Nation	17th
Density per squar mile	98.5
Number of Representatives in Congress	8
Capital City	Nashville
Population	447,877
Rank in State	2nd
Largest City	Memphis
Population	623,530
Number of Cities over 10,000 Population	30
Number of Counties	95

---

* Based on 1970 census statistics compiled by the Bureau of the Census.
† Estimated by Bureau of the Census for July 1, 1972.

TENNESSEE

MAP OF CONGRESSIONAL DISTRICTS
OF TENNESSEE

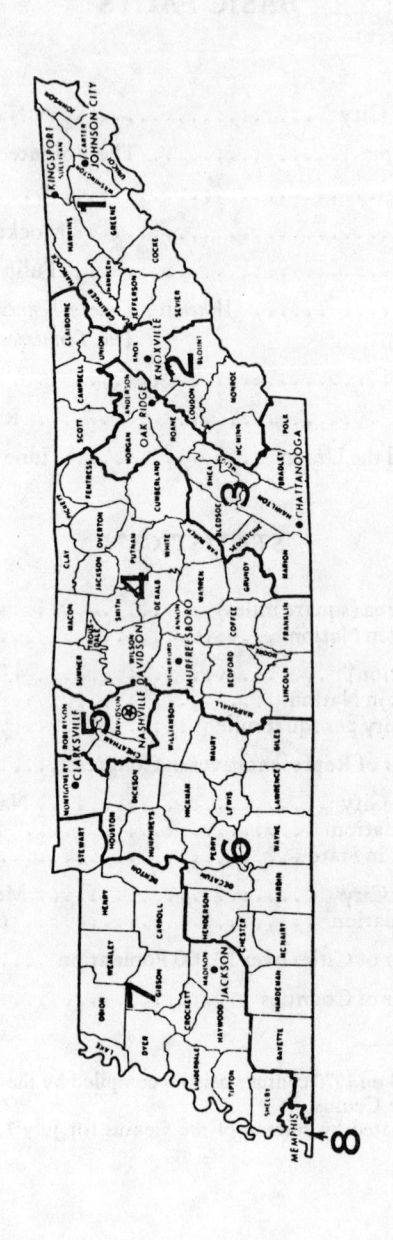

SELECTED BIBLIOGRAPHY

Abernethy, Thomas Perkins. *From Frontier to Plantation; A Study in Frontier Democracy.* Chapel Hill: The University of North Carolina Press, 1932

Alderson, William Thomas and White, Robert H. *A Guide to the Study and Reading of Tennessee History.* Nashville: Tennessee Historical Commission, 1959.

Caldwell, Joshua William. *Studies in Constitutional History of Tennessee.* Cincinnati: The Robert Clarke Company, 1907, 2nd. ed.

Carpenter, William Henry. *The History of Tennessee, from Its Earliest Settlement to the Present Time.* Philadelphia: Lippincott, Grambo and Co., 1854.

Combs, William Hobart and Cole, William E. *Tennessee, A Political Study.* Knoxville, Tenn.: University of Tennessee Press, 1940.

Hale, William Thomas and Merritt, Dixon L. *History of Tennessee and Tennesseeans.* Chicago and New York: The Lewis Publishing Company, 1913. 8 vols.

Folmsbee, Stanley John, Corlew, Robert E. and Mitchell, Enoch L. *History of Tennessee.* New York: Lewis Historical Publishing Company, 1960. 4 vols.

_____. *Tennessee: A Short History.* Knoxville: University of Tennessee Press, 1969.

Hamer, Philip May, ed. *Tennessee: A History, 1673-1932.* New York: The American Historical Society, Inc., 1933, 4 vols.

Isaac, Paul E. *Prohibition and Politics: Turbulent Decades of Tennessee.* Knoxville: University of Tennessee Press, 1965.

Moore, John Trotwood and Foster, Austin P. *Tennessee: The Volunteer State, 1769-1923.* Chicago, Nashville: The S. J. Clarke Publishing Co., 1923, 4 vols.

NAME INDEX

Adams, John, 13
Adams, John Quincy, 20
Anderson, Joseph, 6
Arthur, Gabriel, 1

Baker, Howard H., Jr., 28
Bate, William B., 22
Bedford, Captain, 7
Bell, John, 14
Benton, Thomas Hart, 12
Blanton, Ray, 29
Bledsoe, Abraham, 7
Blount, William, 3, 4, 5, 8
Boone, Daniel, 5
Bradley, Edward, 13
Bragg, Braxton, 18
Brown, Aaron V., 15
Brown, John C., 20
Brown, Neill S., 15
Browning, Gordon, 26
Brownlow, William G., 18, 19
Bryan, William Jennings, 25
Buchanan, John P. 22

Campbell, George Washington, 7, 8
Campbell, William B., 16
Cannon, Newton, 12, 13
Caroline, Queen of England, 16
Carroll, William, 10, 12
Carter, Jimmy, 29
Charleville, Charles, 1
Cheatham, Edwin S., 17
Chester, Robert I., 21
Claiborne, William Charles Coles, 6
Clark, William, 14
Clay, Henry, 20
Clement, Frank G., 27, 28
Cocke, William, 5
Coffee, John, 13
Cooper, Prentice, 26

Cox, John I., 23
Crockett, David, 15
Cumberland, William Augustus, Duke of, 1, 16

Darrow, Clarence, 25
Davidson, William Lee, 3
Decatur, Stephen, 15
De Kalb, Johann, 13
DeSoto, Hernando, 1
Dickinson, Jacob M., 23
Dickson, William, 6
Dunn, Winfield, 28
Dyer, Richard Henry, 10

Eaton, John H., 12
Ellington, Bufford, 27, 28

Fontess, James, 11
Foote, A. H., 17
Ford, Gerald R., 29
Forest, Major General, 18
Franklin, Benjamin, 8
Franzier, James B., 22, 23

George II, King of England, 16
Gibson, John, 11
Giles, William Branch, 8
Grainger, Caleb, 5
Grainger, Mary, 5
Grant, Ulysses S., 17, 18
Gray, Frank, Jr., 29
Greene, Nathanael, 3
Grundy, Felix, 13, 15

Hall, William, 12
Hamblen, Hezekiah, 19
Hamilton, Alexander, 9
Hancock, John, 15
Hardemann, Thomas Jones, 11
Hardin, Joseph, 9
Harris, Isham G., 17
Harrison, William Henry, 14
Hawkins, Alvin, 21
Hawkins, Benjamin, 3

Hayes, Rutherford B., 21
Haywood, John, 11
Henderson, James, 10
Henderson, Richard, 2
Henry, Patrick, 10
Hood, J. B., 18
Hooper, Ben W., 23
Horton, Henry H., 25
Houston, Samuel, 11, 20
Hull, Cordell, 26
Humphreys, Parry Wayne, 8

Jackson, Andrew, 6, 10, 11, 12, 14
Jefferson, Thomas, 4, 10, 14
Johnson, Andrew, 16, 18, 19
Johnson, Cave, 12, 15
Joliet, Louis, 1
Jones, James C., 14
Jones, Thomas M., 18

Kay, David M., 21
King, Martin Luther, Jr., 28
Knox, Henry, 4

LaSalle, Robert Cavalier, Sieur de, 1
Lauderdale, James, 12
Lawrence, James, 8
Lewis, Meriwether, 14, 15
Lincoln, Abraham, 16, 18
Lincoln, Benjamin, 8
Loudon, John Campbell, Earl of, 1
Loudon, John Campbell, 4th Earl of, 19

Macon, Nathaniel, 14
Madison, James, 7, 8, 10, 13
Malone, Dudley Field, 25
Marion, Francis, 8

Marks, Albert S., 21
Marquette, Jacques, 1
Marshall, John, 13
Maury, Abram, 7
Maynard, Horace, 21
McAllister, Hill, 25
McCord, Tim Nance, 26
McMillin, Banton, 22
McMinn, Joseph, 8
McNair, John, 10
McReynolds, James Clark, 23
Meigs, Return Jonathan, 13
Monroe, James, 9, 13
Montgomery, James, 4
Moore, William, 20
Morgan, Daniel, 8

Needham, James, 1

Overton, John, 7

Paine, Bishop, 20
Patterson, Malcolm R., 23
Peay, Austin, 24, 25
Pedro, Jan, 1
Perry, Oliver Hazard, 10
Polk, James Knox, 12, 14
Porter, James D., Jr., 20
Presley, Elvis, 29
Putnam, Israel, 14

Raleigh, Sir Walter, 1
Rhea, John, 7
Rickett, H. L., 21
Roane, Archibald, 6
Roberts, Albert H., 24
Robertson, James, 2, 3, 5
Roosevelt, Franklin D., 26
Roosevelt, Theodore, 23
Rosencrans, William S., 18
Rutherford, Griffith, 6
Rye, Thomas C., 24

NAME INDEX

St. Clair, Arthur, 11
Schlesinger, James R., 28
Scopes, John, 24, 25
Scott, Winfield, 16
Senter, Dewitt Clinton, 19
Sevier, John, 3, 4, 6
Shelby, Isaac, 9
Smith, Daniel, 5
Smith, James, 1
Stewart, Duncan, 7
Sullivan, James, 2
Sumner, Jethro, 1

Taft, William Howard, 23
Taylor, Alfred A., 24
Taylor, Robert L., 22
Thomas, General, 18
Tipton, Jacob, 11
Trousdale, William, 16, 19
Turney, Peter, 22

Van Buren, Martin, 13, 14, 15

Walker, Thomas, 1
Warren, Joseph, 7
Washington, George, 2, 4, 9
Wayne, Anthony, 9
Weakley, Robert, 11
White, John, 7
Williamson, Hugh, 5
Wilson, Daniel, 5
Wilson, Woodrow, 23
Wright, Frances, 11
Wright, Luke E., 23

HOUSTON PUBLIC LIBRARY

R01 0649 3776